Elder & Sage Community Gardens
An Urban Uprising

Clare Hanrahan
Celtic Wordcraft Books, Asheville, North Carolina

Published by Celtic Wordcraft Books
Hanrahan.celticwordcraft@gmail.com
celticwordcraftavl.wordpress.com
https://www.facebook.com/PageAveAVL

ISBN: 979-8-218-88479-6

Cover design: Lynch Graphics, Inc.
Interior design: Andy Reed, Pisgah Press

Printed in the USA 2026

What Readers are Saying

"A vivid and powerful portrait of an important community project. A reminder of what community working together can grow in the unlikeliest of places."

—David Forbes, editor, journalist, *The Asheville Blade*.

"Anyone who has ever set foot in Elder & Sage Gardens and experienced its magic will gain an even deeper appreciation for it thanks to this detailed account. For nine years, flora have flourished here in spite of gravel and concrete, urban toxicity and other uncertainties... Here's hoping for many more verdant years!"

—Carissa Pfeiffer, Librarian, Pack Memorial Library,
Buncombe County Special Collections.

"Having been a professional gardener for much of my life, I've had the pleasure of traveling to and working in many beautiful and amazing gardens. For all that I've seen—from the tropical gardens of Hawaii to the grounds of the Biltmore estate—the Elder & Sage Community Garden stands out for its creative spirit and grassroots community effort."

—Scott Owen, gardener and silversmith

About the Author

Clare Hanrahan has lived in the Asheville area since 1989 and downtown since 2011. She is committed to the work of global justice, peace, and protection of the Earth and reports on demonstrations and marches posting online as Asheville on the Ground.

Other books by Clare Hanrahan include:

Conscience & Consequence: A Prison Memoir, Celtic Wordcraft Books, 2005. ISBN: 978-0-9758846-1-4. Available from LuLu.com, or the author: hanrahan.celticwordcraft@gmail.com

The Half-Life of a Free Radical: Growing up Irish Catholic in Jim Crow Memphis, Celtic WordCraft Books, 2016. ISBN: 978-0-9758846-9-0. Available from IngramSpark Publishing Services, or through the author's website: celticwordcraftavl.wordpress.com.

Acknowledgments

Thanks to friends and family who gave the time out of their busy lives to read early drafts and offer suggestions, corrections and encouragement: Diane Ashworth, Bill Branyon, Arturo Carrillo, David Forbes, Scott Owen, Carissa Pfeiffer, Eileen and Alice Queener, Ann Wilder. Thanks also to Anne Gietzen, a perennial patron of community gardens who helped with production costs; and to Karen Alley with the North Carolina Writers' Network for her early critique.

And to my dear companion Arturo Carrillo—a continual support in the garden and in my life.

As we work to heal the earth, the earth heals us.
—Robin Wall Kimmerer

Table of Contents

Preface

In the name of the bee, And of the butterfly,

And of the breeze, amen!

—Emily Dickinson

A tenacious group of wayside gardeners in Asheville, North Carolina, became the official stakeholders in a blazing hot gravel lot on June 1, 2017. There was not a single leaf or blossom when we first opened the chain link fence, not any of the pleasing scents of lavender, rosemary, and lemon balm, no pollinating bees and butterflies. Only the pigeons roosting on the nearby rooftops, the acrid whiff of car exhaust on the breeze, and the detritus of thoughtless passersby in a city that attracts as many as twelve million visitors annually.

We began as a diverse gathering of neighbors and friends guided by an urgency to reclaim and repurpose a vacant city lot in our downtown neighborhood. Our vision was to transform the gravel-laden ground into a welcoming community garden providing habitat for trees, plants, birds, and beneficial insects, affirming their right to continued existence in our densely developing urban environment.

As a lifelong activist and writer, I have spent much of my seventy-seven years in a state of determined resistance to the global suffering and ecological damage of endless wars and the environmental blindness of rampant development. My journey has taken me through women's shelters and out in the streets to join protests; speaking against militarism and standing for endangered trees, mountains, and rivers; into prison cells and out into wayside gardens.

Prison? Yes. I spent six months confined in Alderson Federal Prison Camp in West Virginia, a consequence of peaceful protest. I have always felt a deep connection with the Earth, so my inmate work assignment was an unexpected blessing. I earned my horticulture certificate in the prison greenhouse. It was a place of connection and refuge from the stress of incarceration.

I learned much more than horticulture in prison. I found common ground living and working among people with varied levels of education, emotional maturity, mental health, and physical ability, as well as ethnic, racial, and cultural diversity. It is much like the work of tending to a garden with all its complex biodiversity and competitive adaptations for survival in an ecosystem long out of balance.

Over the years I have also developed skills with grassroots organizing, but my real strengths are persistence and passion and a deep belief that doing the work in front of us, little by little, is the best way forward. I found a new project in the gravel lot in Asheville.

Elder & Sage was never just a garden. It is a commons—a place where neighbors and tourists meet, where bees buzz around the blossoms, where song sparrows nest in the evergreens. It's a place of learning, of listening, of labor, and an ever-evolving oasis in a concrete and black-top wasteland.

We built raised beds, planted pollinator habitats, and hosted gatherings. We also faced challenges: Conflicts over access, misunderstandings, disagreements, and the slow work of building trust as we learned how to work cooperatively toward a common goal. People serve what they love, and in our gardens that love is evident and reflects the authenticity of life, in all its messiness, its beauty, and its capacity for renewal.

This story is a people's history, one that needs telling. A way to give voice to the efforts of so many to "preserve the integrity, stability and beauty of the biotic community,"[1] as ecologist Aldo Leopold wrote, and to reclaim a small part of what should not be lost as the investors and developers encroach wherever they find advantage.

This book has been germinating over the past decade, taking root as I cultivated the garden. It is a tribute to the people who showed up, the plants that persisted, the trees that pushed up through the gravel. It is a way to share some of the stories that unfolded on our way from gravel to green as we reclaimed space for the precious diversity of the natural world.

> **Ours is not the task of fixing the entire world all at once, but of stretching out to mend the part of the world that is within our reach.**
>
> —Clarissa Pinkola Estes

Elder & Sage Community Gardens:

An Urban Uprising

Clare Hanrahan

CELTICWORDCRAFT

Chapter One
Chronicle of a Changing City

> Tourism is a double-edged sword—always has been and always will be. We benefit, and we pay a price.
>
> —John Boyle, *Asheville Watchdog*

It was, in truth, an act of survival. The suffocating heat radiating from black-top surfaces, the fenced-off gravel lots, and the loss of benches and shade trees turned our neighborhood into an asphalt wasteland. About 250 low-income seniors and people with disabilities live in the Battery Park and Vanderbilt Apartments that flank the public land outside our downtown Asheville homeplace. A drab grey urban desert has replaced the wide lawns and parkland that once graced the grounds of the original Battery Park Hotel. Defying the desolation, we neighbors began to seed the cracks and crevices along the crumbling parking lots and beneath the few struggling urban trees.

The surrounding Blue Ridge Mountains, seen from my thirteenth-floor window in the Battery Park Apartments, impart a deeply felt ancient embrace. Houses cling to the ridge tops and slopes of surrounding mountains and new, box-like hotels steal the views from below. In October of 2025, 1.2 million non-residents visited downtown Asheville, according to the Asheville Downtown Association. Tensions between local needs and the overwhelming impact of this overtourism are rising as fast as the hotels built to accommodate them.

Clamor and Commotion

Today, tour buses and pub cycles—powered by bridal parties or raucous revelers—bring a carnival-like energy to the neighborhood. Throngs of tourists spill out from nearby hotels and crowd the sidewalks walking briskly past unhoused residents sleeping on park benches or in building entryways. On many summer weekends, ticketholders for pricey music concerts line the sidewalks awaiting entry to the civic center known now as Harrah's Cherokee Center. Band followers arrive in vans and campers, living in the parking lots for the duration. Some set up tables and tents to market their wares. Each year high school and community college graduations bring crowds of locals who would otherwise seldom venture downtown. Bobby, our neighborhood sax player, a regular presence outside the civic center, courts the coins of passersby as he blares familiar tunes from the few in his repetitive repertoire.

Food and beer delivery trucks, engines idling, often block the streets. Fire engines, sirens blaring, race through town. Tourist groups pass on foot, on electric bicycles, hoverboards, and buses. Tens of thousands of vehicles stream by in a toxic torrent on the nearby interstates. Clamor and chaos are pervasive as the climate disasters intensify, democracy unravels, and famine, genocide, and wars persist.

In 2020 and 2024, then candidate President Trump held rallies at the Thomas Wolfe auditorium in the civic center. His visits attracted a spectacle of adulation and opposition among the massive crowds. Today frequent rallies against President Trump's policies spill into the streets as chanting demonstrators march through the neighborhood. Others drive through the streets in large and loud trucks brandishing Trump flags to assert their loyalty.

Through it all, rising above the din, the bells of the iconic 1909 Basilica of Saint Lawrence toll—marking the hours with a resonant, melodic tone. Sometimes, they ring out a familiar hymn, summoning me back to my Catholic schoolgirl days for a moment of reflection and grace.

Boom and Bust and Boom Again

Asheville's tourist economy has come, gone, and come again. After the Great Depression, the city suffered "years of neglect, deterioration, and functional obsolescence."[2] The rapid growth of previous decades had burdened the city with massive debt until 1976. Two prestigious downtown hotels were unable to withstand the economic collapse. The nine story George Vanderbilt Hotel that opened in 1924, closed in 1969. The Battery Park Hotel followed in 1979. Both became federally subsidized housing for low-income seniors and people with disabilities at a time when much of the downtown area was struggling.

In late 1980, a "revitalization committee" backed by the Chamber of Commerce, the *Asheville Citizen*, WLOS-TV and others, including the Mayor and City Council, put forth an ill-conceived plan for an indoor shopping mall and hotel. They proposed to use eminent domain law to raze eleven city blocks, bulldozing eighty-five aging downtown buildings. Within a week, many small business owners, long-time residents, artists and newcomers joined together to resist the destruction. The group, "Save Downtown Asheville," deployed many creative ways to awaken the public to the extent of the proposed demolitions. An art installation called "The Wrap" was the brilliant idea of Asheville native Peggy Gardner. Along with 200 supporters, they wrapped the perimeter blocks with sheets to visually mark the threatened buildings. The group was successful in defeating the bond referendum that would have financed the devastation.[3] A similar visual demonstration has been used recently by residents and neighbors opposed to the proposed destruction by UNC Asheville of a beloved forty-five-acre urban forest near downtown Asheville.[4]

By the time I arrived in the neighborhood in 2011, the tourist economy was booming again, and hotel developers were looming. I was 62 and officially an "elder" when I moved into the Battery Park Apartments. My home occupies a small section of the penthouse where the legendary entrepreneur Edwin W. Grove once lived and died. It was the second of two hotels bearing the same name and built upon Stony Hill, a high, densely wooded knoll once used as Cherokee hunting ground.

During the American Civil War, this high point of Asheville held a defensive artillery battery, hence the name of the subsequent hotels. The original 1886 Queen Anne–style Battery Park hotel was burned and demolished in 1923, and much of the hill where it stood was levelled. Grove replaced the demolished hotel with a thirteen-story brick and limestone edifice, an architectural mix of neoclassical and Spanish romanticism.

When Grove died in 1927, construction was halted on the Grove Arcade Public Market. It was finally completed in 1929, occupying a full city block across from the Battery Park hotel, but not as the planned seventeen-story skyscraper.

In 1942 the federal government occupied the Arcade for the duration of World War II. My just-married father, a tech sergeant in the U.S. Army Air Corps weather intelligence division, was stationed there during the war—a bit of family history I only came to know after moving in across the street. The building was later reclaimed by the city and the restored Arcade opened in late 2002 with shops, restaurants, offices and 42 luxury apartments.

Tour guides regularly pass through the neighborhood. They enthrall visitors with stories of ghosts and murders at the Battery Park Hotel, and of the history of E. W. Grove and the many famous people who once stayed here, among them the literary giants F. Scott Fitzgerald and Thomas Wolfe. We have our own artists, poets, authors, musicians and other interesting personages living here today, and if ghosts of past years are still roaming, I have yet to see one.

A Neighborhood in Transition

> The gentry are all around, on each side they are found.
> Their wisdom's so profound, to cheat us of our ground.
> Stand up now, stand up now.
>
> Leveller song, 1640s

Local artist and environmentalist Ron Ogle is my neighbor at the Battery Park Apartments. His 2004 landscape oil titled *The View That Made Asheville Famous* depicts part of the breathtaking mountain vistas seen from the veranda of the original Battery Park Hotel. It is displayed in the Pack Memorial Library. The view, still visible from our roof-top porch, looks west "towards that 13-mile distant narrow river cleft canyon through which modern folk travel on Interstate 40 all the way to Tennessee."[5]

In 2009 the Hotel Indigo intruded on this panoramic vista. The uninspired twelve-story building became the first downtown hotel built in over two decades, replacing the Chamber of Commerce building on Haywood Street. Numerous more old buildings would soon fall to the wrecking ball.

In 2014, The Flying Frog restaurant on Haywood Street—an Asheville institution for nearly two decades—was demolished, along with an adjacent city-owned parking garage that had long stood vacant, serving as a nuisance habitat for rats. Faux stone retaining walls and a chain-link fence rendered the land hostile, and it soon came to be known as the "Pit of Despair," a no-man's land where environmentalists had fought developers and the city council to a glaring standstill.

Years before, the Basilica of Saint Lawrence had torn down a small annex building and expanded its black-top surface parking. Then in 2015, a two-story brick building on Page Avenue—once a hardware store and later leased by the Sister Cities nonprofit—was demolished. The city claimed it was cheaper to tear it down than to repair the leaking roof and damaged electrical wiring. In its place, yet another graveled, fenced, and vacant lot scarred the neighborhood, posted with "No Trespassing" signs.

That same year, developers of the Cambria Suites Hotel tore down the old brick edifice that was once home to Kosta Men's Wear and a Subway restaurant. They also killed several mature trees and removed the park bench beneath them. The unsightly twelve-story tourist lodging was built right across from the Grove Arcade Public Market.

The builders used the vacant lot on Haywood Street across from the Vanderbilt Apartments as a staging area for hotel construction equipment. Neighbors posted our objections on the fence. In response, the construction superintendent, Chris Bauer, built a garden bench and a planter and placed it in front of the fenced lot. The gesture was kind but did little to relieve the impact of all the destruction and hotel construction in the neighborhood.

In my 2015 article "Tear down that fence" in the *Asheville Citizen-Times*[6] I lamented the very real hardships imposed on our elder residents whose interests and concerns are seldom considered when making plans for the best use of nearby public land. Life persists even in the harshest places, and so did we.

Chapter Two
Putting the Park Back in Battery Park

> There are no unsacred places; there are only sacred
> places and desecrated places.
>
> —Wendell Berry

Asheville residents have long advocated for a park on the last remaining public land in the Downtown Historic District. The Basilica of Saint Lawrence, the Pack Memorial Library, Harrah's Cherokee Center, and the Grove Arcade Public Market are part of the neighborhood.

The city bought this land in 2003 so a developer could build a fifteen-story structure along with a five-story parking deck that would wrap around the Battery Park Apartments. In 2005, Battery Park Apartment neighbors and allies united to defeat the proposal. Many, including longtime resident Roger Smith, meticulously gathered signatures on a petition to "protect this area for future use as a civic plaza, public park, and cultural center." I joined the effort in 2014.

Plant Trees, Not Cars!

That summer, artist and activist Coleman Smith crafted a series of hand-held signs reading "I Support a Park Here" and "Plant Trees, Not Cars." I began an online photo essay, posting scores of images on my Facebook account of neighbors, passersby, and tourists holding the signs aloft, with each post receiving dozens of "likes."

Coleman and I are old friends. We were part of the successful local effort in 2008 that saved the century-old magnolia tree planted by philanthropist George Willis Pack who donated the land in perpetuity to the people. The revered tree was threatened to be cut and the public land sold off for a condominium project on City-County Plaza.[7]

Over the years, Coleman and I were active in many anti-war and environmental justice efforts on both local and national levels. We traveled throughout the southeast region documenting and speaking about the environmental impacts of militarism. The work of building a community garden would be a welcome respite from the soul-troubling realities we encountered in our research and travels. Saving one small parcel of desecrated land would be a tangible and achievable means to bring hope and healing.

Our direct actions were gaining attention. The local Asheville weekly, *Mountain Xpress*, dispatched reporter Virginia Daffron to interview neighbors. In 2015 she wrote, "This Bud's for You – Grassroots campaign cultivates beauty, community,"[8] an article that encouraged us to continue our efforts. As our neighbor Carol Hubbard told her, "I have a relationship with these scraggly little plants, even in these tiny places, the sacredness of the earth must be acknowledged."

Award winning poet, the late Barbara Gravelle—a lifelong resident of Western North Carolina and park advocate told the reporter, "From the roof garden of the Battery Park where I live, I see this ugly scar. A park here will add class to the city." Barbara became an early and enthusiastic garden supporter. Although she did not live to see a public park here, her legacy of community service remains a part of this neighborhood story. Others stepped forward to make a public stand, including local singer-songwriter David LaMotte, who joined neighbors and friends in a lively musical demonstration across from the Basilica.

Downtown resident and civic activist, Charlie Thomas, organized "Friends of Saint Lawrence Green," a citywide initiative of People Advocating Real Conservancy (PARC). The group circulated a petition titled Imagine Saint Lawrence Green calling for a public park on the vacant city land across from the Basilica of Saint Lawrence. In December 2015, PARC presented the petition to the Asheville City Council with over 4,000 signatures. In 2017, former City Councilman Cecil Bothwell wrote, "We who've worked and fought to establish a park on this site for more than a decade have collected thousands of signatures to that effect. Where are the petitions for retail stores and a high rise?"[9]

These efforts helped stave off proposals for private development. Yet despite the expressed will of the people, the asphalt wasteland remains. Park critics warned of excessive tax expenditures for design and maintenance. In my opinion piece, I proposed: "Bring in Asheville's garden clubs, the vegetable vendors, the nonprofit groups focused on greening the city, the permaculture activists, the herb lovers and plant people who could make a fine community green space for very little money."[10]

Many studies show that urban green space mitigates the heat islands created by asphalt surface-parking while enhancing the social connections so vital to mental and emotional health. Over the years it has taken the determined and continued efforts of concerned residents to protect and preserve Asheville from too many ill-advised and unsustainable proposals.

A Gorgeous Insurgency

> The passion to produce is very great. One man, who has not yet been assigned his little garden plot, is hopefully watering a jimson weed simply to have something of his own growing.
>
> — John Steinbeck

While developers, citizens and city government squabbled over best use of open spaces, a few determined neighbors nurtured the tenacious and nutritious plants bravely pushing through the concrete. We found hope in those strong plants, the golden dandelion, the red clover, and the blue-blossomed chicory. We added a cup of soil here, a little seedling there, and decorated the reclaimed earth with whimsical ceramic figurines. It was, as the late poet Maxine Kumin wrote, "the gorgeous insurgency of these smart green weeds."

We salvaged bricks from the demolished building that once stood at the corner of Page Avenue and Battery Park and placed them around the small squares of bare earth beneath the few remaining sidewalk trees. There we planted more seeds. We trained morning glories up the tree trunks and hung wind chimes from the branches. We named ourselves Elder & Sage for the healing plants we hoped would soon have a place to thrive.

Day after day our intrepid group of wayside gardeners continued, doing what we could to nurture life in every little patch of earth along the perimeter of the gravel and asphalt lots. We decided that we would work all the edges until we could move into the center. Our friend Scott Owen, a lifelong gardener, referred to our efforts as "an occupation of herbs and flowers." Soon, violets and snapdragons, marigolds and pansies had replaced the litter, the cigarette butts, and the dog waste. Coleman built a long planter box that we placed along the edge of the crumbling parking lot on Page Avenue. We called in other friends to bring more soil and plants.

I rescued iris bulbs from the grounds of the former Three Brothers restaurant on Haywood Street, bulldozed in 2014 after 54 years as a family restaurant. We planted those heirloom bulbs in our new sidewalk garden box, eager to see the magnificent purple blooms come again.

The Hyatt Place Hotel, later known as the Double Tree by Hilton, took the place of that long-time neighborhood dining space. It was hard to witness such wanton destruction for what my old friend Bill Branyon has called "the impersonal, corporate juggernauts of money extraction."

Our neighbor, the late Edwin Gonzales, had been nurturing the rooftop garden at Battery Park Apartments[11] for years, bringing us some of the color and beauty of his Puerto Rico homeland where he said the flowers bloomed on porches and balconies everywhere in the urban areas. I would often find him singing as he tended the plants, and he shared his knowledge gladly. It was a sad and difficult day in 2017 when a new building manager arrived at Battery Park Apartments and ordered the garden removed. The rationale had something to do with her fear of water leaks. It was a devastating blow.

But true gardeners are not so easily deterred. Like the seeds sprouting in the cracks and crannies throughout the neighborhood, gardeners are always looking for another space to nurture beauty. Edwin was soon at work building a large planter box. Many of Edwin's special flowers that once graced the Battery Park Apartments rooftop porch would later thrive in our community gardens. The construction boom was in full swing and so were we.

Scott and Coleman, both long-time community activists, recognized the needs we were working to address. They brought two homemade benches that we placed along the sidewalks across from our apartment buildings so our elder neighbors could have a nearby place to sit and visit outside. The city had removed too many benches from the neighborhood in an effort that seemed intended to discourage occupancy by the unhoused among us.

"Forgive Us Our Trespasses"

> The violets in the mountains have broken the rocks.
>
> —Tennessee Williams

It was a rainy, chilly morning in early April 2017 when students in the Environmental and Social Justice Crew at Warren Wilson College, along with their professor, boldly unloaded a truck full of soil between the sidewalk and the fenced-off lot on Page Avenue. With shovels in hand, we spread the rich soil and with seeds and plants from Ivy Creek Family Farm, we transformed the sterile ground into a fertile space for life. Though the "No Trespassing" sign still hung on the fence, we knew the seeds we planted that day would know no bounds.

Back at Warren Wilson College, Sydney Grange presented her research paper, Our Backyard: Community Engagement in Local Land Use Decisions, and we were all invited. Her thesis called for a "binding Community Benefits Agreement" in development affecting local neighborhoods. The encouragement of these students showed we were gaining support from those who understood the value of intergenerational connection and community engagement for the common good.

Coleman, our early mainstay, brought more hand-crafted wooden planter boxes to place along the fence, along with another truckload of soil and a load of bricks he salvaged with his son Trevor from a building being demolished in West Asheville. Anne Gietzen, a local gardener and volunteer with the Buncombe Fruit and Nut Club, gifted a wide variety of flowers and herbs, including our first elderberry bush, and Martha Grist brought a huge planter of sage. These herbal namesakes of the Elder & Sage Community Gardens would now become a living presence in the neighborhood. With so much help, we were building the foundations to nourish ourselves and our environment. Neighbors were beginning to take notice.

Permission Granted: One year at a Time

> Gardening is the most therapeutic and defiant act you can do, especially in the inner city. Plus you get strawberries.
>
> —Ron Finley, L.A. Green Grounds

In late April of 2017, our opportunity to expand arrived. The City of Asheville's Office of Sustainability announced the availability of four city lots for temporary use by garden groups as part of their Asheville Edibles program. One was the vacant gravel lot on Page Avenue at Battle Square where we had been planting along the perimeter fence. At one-tenth of an acre, about the size of a basketball court, it is a prime center-city lot bordered on one side by a two-story brick building that once housed The Captain's Bookshelf, and on the opposite with black-top surface parking. The front opens to Page Avenue and faces both the Grove Arcade and the Battery Park Apartments. The rear opens to a back alley leading to a hotel parking garage. It is an accessible and highly visible location.

On hearing the good news, I applied on behalf of our garden group. In the application I explained our intent: As an elder-led effort to bring life and beauty back to our neighborhood, we envisioned creating a place where neighbors could come together to cultivate organic vegetables and native culinary and medicinal herbs—attracting songbirds, butterflies, and bees. Our venture to "green the commons" would offer accessible raised beds, wheelchair-friendly paths, and a spirit of inclusion as an expression of our unique community identity and spirit.

Finally, after some confusion and back-and-forth with officials, the city granted temporary use of the vacant lot for the first year, with a year-to-year possibility of renewal. Amber Weaver, the City's Chief Sustainability Officer, proved to be an accessible and understanding ally.

But this was only the beginning. Even though there was no fee required for our garden group to use the lot, there was no ongoing financial support. The work before us was daunting. Our group was entirely responsible for development, construction, upkeep, watering, and overall maintenance of the garden. Tom Downing, city Compliance Specialist whittled down the pages of the rules and procedures in the garden's Use Agreement to a more reasonable size. I signed the Use Agreement on behalf of our garden group, and together with a handful of willing neighbors, we accepted the challenge.

Chapter Three
Start Where You Are. Use What You Have. Do What You Can

Age is no time to wade in the shallows but to dive deeper into life and take risks for the common good.

—Parker Palmer

And so, we began. In nature mutualistic relationships contribute to species survival and ecosystem resilience. It was a principle I hoped would inspire our organizing efforts, as we worked together in a spirit of service to help restore some measure of ecological balance to our urban neighborhood.

The shared labor of community gardening would take us out of our small apartments and into the center of life in our dynamic city. Here we could cultivate friendships with a wider community, connect with tourists, business owners, restaurant and construction workers, with our well-to-do neighbors, and the housed and unhoused poor. All the while growing a little bit of food to nourish our bodies, and flowers that would nourish our spirits, attract bees and butterflies, and add pleasant scents to the afternoon breeze.

We were confident that a community garden here would benefit not only our neighborhood but also contribute to the biodiversity that sustains a healthy city.

The naysayers were not silent. "You're wasting your time," some said. Others warned, "That land is too valuable to the city. They won't let you keep it long enough to grow a tomato." Some watched from a distance with a "wait and see" attitude, unsure of what we were up to. I posted announcements in both the Vanderbilt and Battery Park Apartments inviting participation, and soon even some of the early skeptics were asking, "How can we help?"

We were not at all alone in trying to reclaim nature from urban blight and developmental disasters. We had a lot to learn, and many good examples of successful urban gardens. Asheville Botanical Garden, a native plant preserve on ten acres adjacent to the University of North Carolina, has been around for 65 years. It's a living assembly of rare and endangered species, and an ongoing inspiration.

Mountain Area Gardeners in Community (MAGIC), active from 1983 until spring of 2000, organized and supported "as many as 13 community gardens outside of schools, housing projects, homeless shelters and other spots throughout the city," according to a story in the *Mountain Xpress*.[12] Roberta Greenspan, an old-time fiddler, bicyclist and gardener, offered me space to get my hands in the soil in a small plot on the corner of Central Avenue at Clayton Street. It was my first experience with a community garden.

The legacy of MAGIC is carried forward today through the work of Bountiful Cities. Since 2000, they have cultivated partnerships with community gardens, school gardens, and edible parks throughout Asheville and Buncombe County.

Before we had our own neighborhood space to garden, I met Joan Pinegar, then the Garden Coordinator at Isaac Dickson Elementary School. Joan shared her knowledge and donated plants and seeds for our early efforts to green our neighborhood. Joan is now director of The Educational Garden Project and The Garden Camp for Kids, helping children fall in love with nature by providing "places of engagement with the natural, living world."

Shortly after we began Elder & Sage, Treska Lindsey, then in her nineties, came by to show her support. Treska founded a community garden that was maintained by the residents of Aston Park Tower public housing for nearly twenty years. These connections, rooted in the rich legacy of Asheville's urban gardeners, nourish our efforts, much as supportive mother trees send out nutrients to nearby saplings, encouraging growth.

Design and Build

> The great social justice changes in our country have happened
> when people came together, organized, and took direct action.
>
> —Dolores Huerta

We created the Elder & Sage Community Gardens from the gravel up, the design unfolding as materials and helping hands became available. The city asked for a design plan, so our steadfast volunteer Coleman drafted an impressive and professional document. We were well on our way gathering materials, building walkways and garden boxes from donated and scrap lumber, hauling soil and planting seeds. Our volunteer crew of two, sometimes three carpenters went to work right away.

Ponkho Bermejo, a co-director with BeLoved Community, delivered several planter boxes he had built and painted with the theme: "Start where you are. Use what you have. Do what you can." That sentiment expressed our approach to the daunting task of transforming a gravel lot into a garden. Ponkho spent days dismantling discarded pallets and laying our initial walkway over the gravel to make an accessible path inside. He used the remnants of the pallets to craft a colorful tear-drop shaped planter that became an art centerpiece for years until it was claimed by rain and weather.

BeLoved works throughout the county to end local homelessness, poverty, and racism. When other commitments called Ponkho away, Coleman completed the wooden path to the back gate, working through the Christmas holiday that year. He also installed the front entry gate and built long worktables in the back corner. Coleman has moved on to other projects, but his foundational help was vital to garden development.

The completion of the wooden pathway through the garden provided access to the planter box for our neighbor Amanda LaVesque, an award-winning artist and actor, who depends on a wheelchair to make her way around town. Every year she and her mother Patty plant vegetables and herbs in their planter at the front of the garden built by her neighbor Alan.

Amanda inspires us all, adapting and thriving in the face of challenge, as do the many plants finding their niche in our urban gardens.

We have no electricity on site, so building garden boxes was a slow process. We accomplished much of the work off site, sometimes in the small apartments of our neighbors. When Coleman discovered an electrical outlet in the vacant public lot across the alley, he plugged in a long extension cord to facilitate the work. We only needed a few hours to cut some thick boards. Soon I received a call. There was a complaint from the Strategic Development Office in the city. "Surely the city can spare a little electricity?" I responded, explaining that we were constructing the garden boxes so our elder neighbors could have a place to plant their seeds. "We have a few dollars left in our treasury and will be happy to reimburse the city if this has strained the budget." We finished cutting the boards, unplugged, and heard no further complaints.

There were many creative solutions to our need for raised beds. Bradley Jones, active with the Food Liberation Front, delivered six half-barrel planters filled with hardy garden perennials, including Jerusalem artichokes (Helianthus tuberosus), horseradish (Armoracia rusticana), and rhubarb (Rheum rhabarbarum). Each container had a code affixed to the side. When captured with a smart phone it opened to an on-line site with information on how to care for the plant. Those plants have survived and still have a place in our bio-diverse gardens. Food liberation is part of a global food sovereignty movement promoting "policies to ensure rights to healthy and culturally appropriate food, produced through ecologically sustainable methods."[13]

Another creative volunteer, Mark Ritzenthaler from the Vanderbilt Apartments, obtained twenty food grade barrels, cutting them into half-barrel planters He fitted each with a water reservoir in the bottom. Bountiful Cities helped with materials costs. The bright blue planters have provided space for cultivation of a variety of vegetables and herbs and are perfect for gardeners who only want to tend a few plants. Grouped together, they make an attractive cluster for companionable plantings.

As our community of plants grew, from a few containers to an impressive variety filled with native perennials and vegetables, so did our community of volunteers.

The late Joe Wakefield, an Asheville native then in his mid-nineties, became a familiar presence in the gardens. He was known around town as "the birdhouse man." He donated several of his creations to the gardens. His Vanderbilt apartment served as a functional carpentry shop. His tools were meticulously organized in a large closet, his table saw was in the living room, and shelves all around were filled with his uniquely designed bird houses.

Before our many volunteer trees pushed up through the gravel to offer shade, we were already feeling the dangerous heat. Monica Tilou gifted a large open-sided canopy to provide rain and sun protection. It was a great afternoon when a dozen volunteers worked together to raise the roof, providing our first "front porch" seating area. This was not to be our last sun shelter. We have lost quite a few due to high wind and the burden of sudden downpours. A sturdier shelter would have eliminated the continual expense, but the Use Agreement stipulates no permanent structures.

A Budding Romance

This story would not be complete without mentioning an unexpected romance that blossomed in the gardens. Arturo Carrillo was an ally from our first days, always encouraging my efforts to green the neighborhood. It seemed he was around at every stage of the process, showing up to help in small ways until he found his niche as garden maintenance manager. In time, as we labored together, our affections deepened. Arturo had never tended a garden before, but soon he was growing a variety of herbs that he used in family recipes from his childhood in Ecuador. Arturo settled in Asheville about twelve years ago. He said the mountains here remind him of his Quito homeland. He has many fascinating stories to tell of his earlier life dancing Salsa with the best

Latin bands in New York City, as a cook in fine restaurants throughout the country, and working with the horses at the historic racetrack in Hialeah, Florida, and in Chicago at the former Arlington Park Jockey Club. Although he is fluent in English, he often greets and converses with our many Latino visitors in his native tongue, adding a welcoming multi-cultural ambiance to our gardens.

One summer Arturo and I were enjoying a quiet Sunday morning in the gardens when Elizabeth Eubanks stopped by for a visit. She is the lead gardener at From the Ground Up, a community garden located under an overpass in downtown Pensacola, Florida. The garden she stewards is part of Innisfree Hotels' Hive Foundation, "a corporate social responsibility initiative aimed at promoting sustainability, philanthropy, and local community impact." She interviewed both Arturo and me as she filmed the gardens. The video sometimes pops up on YouTube.[14] It is always a joy to meet such a kindred spirit and to learn about the corporate support she receives for her community garden. The Hive Foundation is a good example many Asheville hotels could consider.

Our accessible wooden pathways, which served us so well in the first few years, over time gave way to the feet of thousands of visitors passing through the gardens. They became a trip hazard when the weathered wood warped. Bountiful Cities provided funds to purchase clay pavers, and Arturo and I took on the enormous job of pulling up all the wood. Fellow community gardener Joe Fioccola, who tends the WECAN Community Garden in the West End Clingman Avenue neighborhood, stopped in on his routine walk about town. He stayed to help finish the labor-intensive task. We saved what we could of the lumber to repurpose for building and repairing garden boxes and advertised the rest for free pickup. Becky and her daughter Ashely came all the way from their farm in Marion. "The boards are just what we needed to finish our chicken coop," they told us. These women, accustomed to hard work, in short order had loaded their truck with the remnant pieces, saving us the labor of hauling the scrap wood away.

Arturo supervised the laying of pavers. He called on his much younger friend, local guitarist and cook David Serra, to do the arduous work as our knees were not up to bending to the task. After they completed the job, David and Arturo broke out into a happy dance to celebrate their accomplishment.

So Much More Than Dirt

> It is impossible to have a healthy and sound society
> without a proper respect for the soil.
>
> —Peter Maurin

We needed soil to fill the many garden boxes that our carpenter friends had built. So, we put out the call. Weeks after we opened the fence, our neighbor Cynthia Sampson arranged delivery of 500 pounds of composted soil from credits she had accumulated with the service Compost Now. Cynthia and her little blind rescue dog are often out and about picking up litter and cigarette butts as they walk along, a task she took on years before the Downtown Improvement District hired "Ambassadors" to do the job.

The vegetable waste collected from our kitchens is transformed into rich and fertile soil, and then into the nutritious food and healing herbs we cultivate. Responsibly managing a compost pile in our urban location was a task we did not have the volunteer capacity to keep up with, so the gift of compost credits has made all the difference.

Contributions of soil and organic fertilizers continued, year after year. Lee Thonus, a river conservationist and community garden ally, delivered a truck load of boxed composted manure from a local horse farm. He has shared this valuable soil nutrient with other community gardens including the Lucy S. Herring Elementary School Peace Garden. We're grateful to the horses and their keepers Gands to Lee's labor for their vital part in the cycle of life.

When Danny's Dumpster donated a hill of soil after I called to inquire about prices, Cindy Gray joined Arturo and me to shovel the soil from the alley into our bin inside the gates. We were relieved when a group of strong young tourists from Boston came along at just the right moment and offered to finish the task. It is part of the magic of this co-creative effort that our ongoing needs are met by so many generous people.

Every year we are blessed with unexpected gifts of seeds and plants to help cultivate a myriad of savory and aromatic herbs and a variety of vegetables and flowers. In October of our first year, local business Sow True Seed donated organic seeds for our winter garden including mustard greens, spinach, collards, and Brussels sprouts.

A visitor with Seed Programs International donated more seeds as part of the group's mission to provide communities with quality seeds of diverse crops. Another time, a visitor from Ukraine came by with a large assortment of seed packets labeled in both Russian and Ukrainian and illustrated with the plant. With both countries at war and many heritage gardens destroyed, our visitor shared his hope that planting these seeds would be another step toward peace and reconciliation. We have made many meals out of the hardy greens and other vegetables grown from these seeds.

Yet another gift of organic vegetable seeds arrived by mail with this note inside:

> My wife Deb and I very much enjoyed meeting you last week in Asheville. Thank you for sharing your lovely garden with us. As promised, here are some seeds to get you started for Spring. Happy gardening!!
>
> Regards,
> Dave Thompson, Seeds of Change.

Every Drop Counts

> *Water is the driving force of all nature.*
>
> —Leonardo da Vinci

In the early days, access to water was the biggest challenge. We hauled water for the first few months, filling half gallon plastic jugs retrieved from the recycling bins. We loaded the water-filled jugs in wagons, then into the elevators and down, then across the street to our few and struggling thirsty plants. Carol Hubbard, a neighbor and longtime activist with the disability rights community, used her Red Radio Flyer wagon to carry water. Larry Williams and Melvin Smith also became regular water carriers from their Battery Park apartments.

A most welcome surprise came the first week we were open through the kindness of Wisconsin tourists John and Jamee Stanley. After coming upon our garden and seeing our needs, they arranged with Tractor Supply in Weaverville for free delivery of another water tank. They were among the many tourists who have helped us over the years.

When a friend donated a long hose, we asked permission from the management of Battery Park and hooked it up to their outside faucet. We needed to fill the few barrels and containers we had. But this involved snaking the hose across Page Avenue. With all the traffic, it created a dangerous situation.

Melvin used the hose to water the garden daily, with special attention to the small watermelon patch he ambitiously began, despite the limitations of raised-bed gardening. As the summer advanced, so did his vines, snaking across the gravel to claim any open space, somewhat like the developers, gaining a foothold throughout the city. Much to his dismay, I had to call a halt to the hose being dragged across the street, and we also had to contain the spread of the wandering watermelon vines.

We then asked the friendly owners of The Captain's Bookshelf in the building next door if we could fill our barrels and buckets from their outside faucet at the back alley. The owners were nearing retirement, and the building was changing hands. Since 1976, this treasured Asheville bookstore has offered a curated collection of quality books, including rare editions and classics. We were sorry they would soon be gone, and happy they were willing to share the water from the back spigot to keep our gardens hydrated. This too was only a temporary solution. We needed a water source on site if our gardens were to survive the scorching summer.

The city wanted to charge $1,000 to install an on-site spigot. Our garden group, newly formed and with scarce funds, resisted. Before too long, our ally on city council, Cecil Bothwell, convinced the city to waive the installation fee. In the Spring of 2018, the city installed a spigot. We agreed to pay for the water, trusting that the funds would be on hand as needed.

Container gardening has its challenges, and keeping the plants hydrated is a huge task. We've run through numerous hoses, damaged when dragged from box to box across sharp gravel. Thankfully, the brief but most welcome summer rainstorms have cooled many afternoons saving us from the onerous task of watering. Then comes the added work of emptying out any standing water to keep mosquitoes from multiplying.

It is quite a task to haul the hose around, so we fill barrels from the spigot for those who are better able to manage carrying a watering can to their garden spot. We still have no rain catchment set up. The downspout from the adjacent building pours floods of water out into the alley. It would require a refit before we could divert the rainwater to garden use. With building ownership changing hands several times, we have been unable to connect with the right person to give permission.

Many volunteers over the years have helped keep the gardens watered. Montford neighbor Mary Kay Smith has come by on many a sweltering Sunday morning to water. She says she enjoys her interactions with garden visitors. John Pritchard was another helpful soul. He stopped in the garden during the summer of our first year looking for a quiet place to read. He later revealed that he lived in his car parked nearby. He watched me struggling with the hose one afternoon and volunteered to help. He took on the task regularly during that long hot summer. We shared many conversations about life and our philosophies until his journeys took him elsewhere.

Many summer evenings when the garden needs a long drink, I have enjoyed the welcome serenades of familiar street musician Michael John playing outside the Grove Arcade. His trumpet and voice bring us the sounds of "blues, jazz, folk, funk, reggae, swing, tribal and world rhythms."

Gatekeepers and Keyholders

> Do your little bit of good where you are. It's those little bits of good put together that overwhelm the world.
>
> —Desmond Tutu

We had to have trusted gatekeepers and key holders to keep the garden open—an ongoing need, as our agreement with the city requires that the garden is kept locked when no volunteer is present. It was a wise idea. We have had to keep managed access for security and protection, though this boundary is not always respected by the fence-jumping opportunists or understood by the visitors who come to find a locked gate. It is difficult to maintain consistency of hours when volunteers come and go, each with their own reasons and responsibilities that call them away.

Our garden soon became a convenient shortcut, a pass-through between downtown destinations. To discourage this, we designed garden paths to slow down the foot traffic and encourage a more meandering passage through the space, one that would allow visitors to really notice the beauty around them as they walked through.

Early on, we had to make it clear that this was not to be a dog-friendly garden. That stipulation is part of our agreement with the city, but many neighbors and tourists arrived at the gates with pets in tow, large and small. Our neighbors with companion dogs were not all happy with the "No Pet" rule. Though much of Asheville is dog friendly, there is no nearby dog park to accommodate their needs. Some dog owners had long been accustomed to letting their pets urinate along the perimeter of the once-vacant lot, and our new plants were suffering from the practice. I sometimes barked at the dog walkers, while shooing them away. The frequent urination burned the plants, leaving white spots on the once green leaves. Old habits lingered.

Smokers, too, had to be reminded not to light up. The scent of tobacco didn't belong among the basil and bee balm. It became a daily task to patrol the perimeter for cigarette butts tossed by passersby. I remember thinking, if there were a seed embedded in every cigarette butt, we'd have a garden sprouting everywhere.

We've posted signs: "No dogs in the gardens." "No smoking." "No dumping." "No picking without permission." Some read them. Some ignored them. Some pulled them down.

We were learning, together, what it meant to steward a shared space. The gate was more than a physical barrier—it was a symbol of intention. When it was open, it invited community. When closed, it protected what we had nurtured. We had to set some boundaries. It is not easy, especially in a public space that invites curiosity and welcomes community. The garden is not a dog park, not a shortcut, not an overnight camping area, not a storage space for travelers' bundles. There is continual tension between our efforts to provide open access for visitors, and the need for protection of what our community has built. As old friend Bill Branyon has suggested, it's "sort of practical anarchism" or "controlled socialism."

Our neighbor in the Battery Park Apartments, Wanda Lovejoy, became a devoted volunteer in our first few years. She loved being in the garden in the early morning hours. As a talented artist and nature photographer, she beautified the space with her colorful paintings on garden boxes and benches. She often wore shirts and jackets she embroidered with brightly stitched flowers. She also captured the ephemeral blossoms with her stunning photographs. We later prepared a slide show of her photographs and presented it to the city council showing the early and emerging beauty in our community gardens. "As the person who opens the gardens every morning, I am fortunate to be there at a time when the plants are waking up. It's a time of great peace and beauty," she told one interviewer.

Thanks to generous donations, Wanda and I enjoyed visiting Reems Creek Nursery and other garden centers to purchase spring flowering bulbs, roses, and other perennials. She planted tulips, daffodil and narcissus that still brighten the front fence every spring. Wanda and her husband Robert eventually moved to the coast of North Carolina, but their contributions of time and talent in the garden are still with us.

Mark Lawson, a Vanderbilt Apartments neighbor, became another dependable volunteer. His time in the garden started when he dropped by to offer his help in 2018. He was a trusted keyholder and reliable afternoon gatekeeper. He was also an adamant enforcer of the "no dogs" rule, a role that required some vigilance as tourists frequently attempted to pass through the gardens with dogs in tow, despite clear signage.

Mark is also a creative cook and loved to grow and tend many of the herbs he used to season his favorite dishes. He was the first to discover the *epazote* (*Dysphania ambrosioides*) used in seasoning many Mexican bean dishes and introduced me to the beautiful and heat-tolerant climbing vine Malabar spinach (*Basella alba*).

Mark's close friend, the late Glen Burleson, also a native of nearby Yancey County and a long-time gardener, soon joined our efforts. Glen planted a box filled with bright orange daylilies and trained deep purple clematis vines along the fence. He assured us that nature spirits were coming around and that they were happy with our efforts to heal the land. He advised us about planting with the cycles of the moon, though I have yet to incorporate that time-honored Appalachian practice into the gardens. This region is rooted in Cherokee wisdom. The Celtic settlers from Scotland and Ireland also brought their wisdom of the natural world when they settled here, adding to the richness of the indigenous Appalachian culture.

"I used to grow flowers professionally, so this is a continuation of my love of plants," Glen said in an interview with Madeline Hackett, a reporter from WYFF in Greenville, South Carolina.[15] She visited the gardens in the spring of 2020 during the COVID lockdown.

"I've talked to the plants. I believe they're a living, breathing thing, just as we are, and they deserve respect and good care," Glen said.

There is magic in the garden if one listens with an open heart. I often notice when the black crows come and perch high on the light posts in the alley or watch from the roof of the adjacent building. I call back to them to attract their attention and welcome their powerful presence as messengers from another realm.

Larry Williams, an ally from the start, also became a regular garden gatekeeper, delighting visitors with his stories about the garden and how it came to be. Long before the city had returned two benches to their place beneath the sycamore tree on Page Avenue, Larry joined me there with a lawn chair on the sidewalk, helping to hold the ground as a community space.

When they were not out fishing, Larry brought his grandson Tyree to the garden. Together they sowed heirloom seeds in a planter he repurposed from the shell of an old pinball machine discarded by the Asheville Pinball Museum across the street.

Larry always carries "an attitude of gratitude." Like many friends of the gardens, he has great ideas for projects and improvements, though without the volunteer capacity to carry it forward, many good suggestions remain unrealized.

Celebrating Peacemakers

Only in the garden can the world's care and woe fly from my mind and let a little bit of peace settle within.

Early in our first year, Rachael Bliss, our neighbor from Vanderbilt Apartments, took the initiative to install a Peace Pole in the center of the gardens. She dedicated it to Asheville, designated an "International City of Peace" in 2010. The Peace Pole Project is a global initiative that promotes the message "May Peace Prevail on Earth." Our pole displays the sentiment in Cherokee, English, Spanish, and Korean. At the 2018 celebration, NC Representative Susan Fisher read the Peace Proclamation, and documentary film maker Yousef Natsha was honored as Peacemaker of the Year for his work in Hebron with Christian Peacemaker Teams. Ceasar Williams, another Vanderbilt Apartments resident, often brought his guitar to the celebrations, leading everyone in singing John Lennon's peace anthem, "Give Peace a Chance."

Several others who have made significant contributions to peace and justice in our community were honored at these events. Among those were Dr. Lew Patrie of Physicians for Social Responsibility, Asheville native son Jim Brown, and Gerry Werhan of Veterans for Peace, along with anti-nuclear activist Ellen Thomas of Women's International League for Peace & Freedom. The late Said Abdallah, a native of Palestine, and Ponkho Bermejo, a native of Mexico, both received Peacemaker of the Year awards for their cross-cultural efforts to promote peace and justice.

At our 2019 ceremony we were happy to have City Councilman Brian Haynes join us in the gardens to read the Proclamation of Peace. Brian, an Asheville native, has long supported a park in the neighborhood. He also shared his concerns for an end to the wars that contribute massively to ecological devastation and climate disasters.

Working together to nurture life is a potent counter to despair and destruction in these times of global crises. The Peace Pole has been the focal point for many garden gatherings, both on International Day of Peace commemorated on September 21, and Armistice Day on November 11, sponsored by the local Veterans for Peace chapter. We were honored to host both events in the gardens until attendance became too large for our space to accommodate.

Chapter Four
On a Wing and a Prayer

From the very beginning, we had a lot of people willing to put their time and energy into the gardens. But we knew we needed support to keep going, not just financial but the backing of the community to help the city understand the importance of keeping this garden alive.

I launched the Elder & Sage Community Gardens Facebook page[16] in 2017 to share photos and stories depicting our progress. It has served as a record of our work over the years. We also kept a guest book on site and encouraged visitors to share their thoughts. It has been heartening to read their many comments.

Spreading the News

It wasn't just our Facebook marketing that helped spread the word about the great work being done in the garden. Polly McDaniel, a media relations/ communication specialist with the city, was likely responsible for some of the good press coverage we received in our first year. After her retirement she spent a summer gardening with us, adding her gracious touch and skills as a master gardener. Polly once told me that she believed allowing the garden group to cultivate the vacant lot was one of the best decisions the city made.

Mackensy Lunsford, a reporter for the *Asheville Citizen-Times*, wrote a feature story in July 2017, "Elder & Sage Community gardening group nurtures life on a gravel lot."[17] She captured the spirit and determination of our gardening group. Later that year, Tiffany Welsh wrote an article for *Food Life Mag*[18] featuring our garden as the first in the Asheville Edibles program and included photos of the gardens in full bloom with borage, marigold, and daisy brightening our freshly painted planters.

Around that time, we were contacted by Deborah Holt Noel, the host of

NC Weekend and a senior producer at PBS North Carolina. She was filming a program as part of an AARP series on active aging called *Boomers*.[19] The film crew spent the entire day with us, arriving at dawn October 17 to film the sun rising over the gardens from our Battery Park rooftop porch.

Ten of our gardeners agreed to be interviewed, including an early ally, Roy Harris, a community advocate and storyteller who a few years earlier helped launch the Southside Community Garden in his historically Black Asheville neighborhood near the River Arts District. Roy has been a continual friend of the gardens, visiting frequently to share stories from his walks about town, on what he has called his "To Boldly Go Where No Brotha Has Been Before Tour."

Other neighbors and friends also joined us that day, including the late activist and artist Kasha Baxter who brought her friend Reed Todd, known for his iconic, eight-foot cast-iron replica of a flat iron, installed in 1997 on Battery Park Avenue. It has become a downtown Asheville landmark and favorite site for local buskers. Reed donated a whimsical cast-iron bench to the gardens, and Montford neighbor Trudi Glenn provided a cushion for the seat. The artful bench has served as a functional centerpiece ever since.

In 2019 we were featured in a program by Wetbird Productions titled "Community Gardens in the City." It was part of the series *Act Two Stories, Reinventing the Second Act of Life*.[20] Gardening "is just like raising children," gardener Larry Williams told the interviewer. "You know, you kind of get into it. Just watching them grow."

The publicity we received brought even more visitors and supporters. We tried to keep a record, but so many folks dropped by with tools, plants, and garden pots that we couldn't keep up. Every day we would hear from garden visitors how much they appreciate the oasis of life we were creating in the urban hardscape. Often, we would find gifts left at the front gates. Sometimes orphaned plants in need of care, other times boxes of garden decorations and ceramic planters. One morning I arrived to find five life-like clay-sculpted heads arranged in a row at the back fence. Many months later, at a downtown Farmers' Market, I met the artist who was happy to know we appreciated the gift.

In the fall of 2019, we received an encouraging note from the Elisha Mitchell Audubon Society:

> We at Elisha Mitchell Audubon Society support the ongoing existence of the Elder and Sage Community garden. It offers locals and tourists an urban sanctuary with plants, art, and recreational space to gather. Elisha Mitchell Audubon is working on forming a partnership with Elder and Sage to help mobilize our bird-friendly communities initiative while giving them resources to educate visitors on birds and bird conservation. This space offers great value to the community and is only going to continue to grow as a community hub for nature connection, education, and relaxation in an increasingly dense urban setting.
>
> The Board of the Elisha Mitchell Audubon Society, Asheville, NC

I regret that we could not follow through with that very encouraging offer of help. We were busy with so many projects then and still adjusting to the ebb and flow of volunteer energy. Caring for the many birds in need of a safe habitat in our urban neighborhood is yet another area where we could learn so much from such a partnership. Perhaps next year.

Powering the Pollinators

> The world is absurd, but I still cling to its flowers like a
> bee drunk on spring.
> —Luke Levi

Bee City USA began in Asheville, North Carolina, in 2012. We were honored when its founder, local pollinator advocate Phyllis Stiles, visited us at the start of our project.

"Boy, I love this effort," she said in an interview with Blue Ridge Public Radio.[21] "This is what we promote all across the country, starting with Bee City USA here in Asheville, because we believe every patch of land can be pollinator habitat."

In our urban environment of asphalt heat islands, artificial lighting, and pollution, it's a wonder any insect can find their way to the city's fragmented green spaces. Studies show that the warmer micro-climate in the city is driving rapid, evolutionary adaptation in many insects. Urban bees have grown larger, while other insects have been stressed to the limits of survival.

Native plants support many endangered insects that keep the garden buzzing, making the nectar sweeter and the gardens brighter. Defining which plants are truly "native" is complex, but given the reality of climate change, with an ecosystem in constant flux, native plants that have evolved to thrive in local conditions are critical to climate resilient gardening.

We were determined to cultivate a variety of native perennials. In 2020, Linda Wolf, a Vanderbilt neighbor who had lived and worked for years in an intentional community, took on the task of documenting the perennials that qualified us as a pollinator habitat. Over time we added butterfly weed (*Asclepias tuberosa*), blue vervain (*Verbena hastata*), cut-leaf coneflower (*Rudbeckia laciniata*), beardtongue penstemon (*Penstemon digitalis*), late purple asters (*Symphotrichum patens*), black-eyed Susan (*Rudbeckia hirta*), and native milkweed (*Asclepias syriaca*), a host plant and food source for the caterpillar of the endangered monarch butterfly (*Danaus plexippus*). Each year we add others, learning as we go about the marvelous biodiversity of our region.

With the climate changes that are upon us, many insects and plants are also migrating and adapting to better survive. Gardeners too must adapt. We prioritize the plants that will best support native pollinators and those that will thrive in our urban, container-confined gardens. We have welcomed many non-native species as well. The immigrant plants that we tend co-exist with those that have flourished in these mountains for generations. Every season we learn more about the complexity and benefits of biodiversity.

Both beneficial and destructive insects have found their way to our little patch of green. The large and alien-looking Chinese mantis (*Tenodera sinensis)* helps keep garden pests to a minimum. The common green grasshopper (*Omocestus viridulus*) has not come in sufficient numbers to be a problem, but the cabbage white butterfly (*Pieris rapae*) is prolific and its caterpillars, enjoy eating the leaves of broccoli and cabbage. We can pick off the Mexican bean beetles (*Epilachna verivestis*) and allow the small red milkweed bugs (*Lygaeus kalmia*) to feed on the seedheads of the common milkweed along the back fence. Many large bees keep busy sipping the nectar as they move along the narrow purple flower heads of the abundant anise hyssop (*Agastache foeniculum*).

A hive of yellow jacket wasps (*Vespula maculifrons*) has taken up residence in the gardens. One afternoon I was checking for ripe figs and noticed one on a nearly ripe fruit. Certain fig varieties require a wasp for pollination and to provide a nutritious environment for her eggs to develop. This mutually dependent relationship has evolved over millions of years. I discovered the wasp nest the painful way: I was busy chopping up plant debris in a compost barrel when I bumped into a small birdhouse on the fence. Out flew a swarm of yellow jackets. The venomous stings lasted for days. Aggressive though they are, they too have their work to do in the garden and defend their nest vigorously.

In a walk about the garden, one can observe life up close: the house sparrow that swoops in and loudly defends her nest hidden in the evergreen shrub; the praying mantis hiding among the Dahlia blossoms around the Peace Pole, its bulging eyes watching intently; the translucent beauty of the setting sun illuminating leaves and casting a golden glow; the fat worms uncovered beneath a planter, and the vast blueness of the Carolina sky on a clear day. Time slows down.

Weeds Are the Real Survivalists

> Weeds are great travelers; they are, indeed, the tramps of the vegetable world. They are going east, west, north, south; they walk; they fly; they swim; they steal a ride; they travel by rail, by flood, by wind; they go underground, and they go above, across lots, and by the highway.
>
> —John Burroughs (1837–1921)

Weeds are the pioneers in the concrete smothered city. They rise from the gravel and in any crack in the asphalt along the fence line that separates our garden from the crumbling parking lot. Come fall, if left to their own devices, they can be a nuisance to passersby, especially when the seeds of the beggar ticks (*Bidens alba*) attach to pants or sleeves.

The morning glories are also aggressively beautiful. Their vibrant color copies the Carolina blue sky, and they are a familiar and welcome sight each morning. But here too, I let them have their way too long. They have twined up the stalks of the evening primrose (*Oenothera biennis*), just coming into its bright yellow bloom, and up into the branches of the young sycamore trees that have grown tall and are just beginning to show color. The lemon-scented evening primrose blossoms are a favorite of the American goldfinch that visits in early summer.

The hybrid chocolate mint has grown leggy and escaped the fence. Its blossoms still attract the bees, but they lean too far into the parking lot, as does the nutritious nettle (*Urtica dioica*) that is not friendly to the unwary.

Last summer, someone sprayed herbicide across the alley on the upper edge of the "Pit of Despair." It turned the leaves into a sickly brown color in an area favored by dogs and homeless passersby as a place to relieve themselves. It's a sad sight, especially in a "bee city," and directly across from our pollinator-friendly garden. Pulling those few weeds would have taken little time, but sometimes short-sighted decisions prevail when there is no real connection to the land.

Volunteer Diane Ashworth, who doesn't shy away from hard work, joined us in 2025, and we spent a good deal of time clearing the fence line along our garden, uprooting and composting the escapees, to prevent anyone spraying poison again. I am amazed at just how much plant material arises from the border community along the fence line and through the gravel that covers the lot. We chop up as much as possible and keep it for the next season to become a first layer as we fill new planter boxes.

One late summer afternoon I was working with Franco Masci, an experienced landscape gardener. The garden was already full of mature perennials, and some had become way out of hand, including the baptisia or false indigo (*Baptisia australis*), whose sprawling, pea-like vine had rooted deeply in the gravel of the herb bed. In the few years since I planted it there, it had grown to over three feet wide and was choking out the less aggressive plants nearby.

"It's a battle of the weak and the strong in the garden," Franco said as he applied his strength to pulling out the stubborn roots. "You have to decide which ones you want to keep, and pull out the rest, or soon your garden will be overcome." Another perennial beauty that we must keep in check is St. John's Wort (*Hypericum perforatum*). Its golden blossoms can banish a dark mood just looking at them.

Conflicts and Misunderstandings

> Welcoming diversity of opinion and listening closely and compassionately while disagreeing is hard work. Finding ways to collaborate with people we find challenging is tough.
>
> —David LaMotte, author of
> *You Are Changing the World Whether You Like it or Not*[22]

Conflict is an inevitable tension in any organization. At the beginning of our efforts the tension was greater when individual roles and responsibilities were not yet clear to all who came forward. Though it was a love of gardening that brought us together, our differences soon emerged. We held varied political and religious views, conflicting ideas about garden design and concerns about how much space each gardener could have and where their box would be placed. Sometimes in that first summer, with so much work before us, the squabbles felt like schoolyard power plays, especially among some of the men, each with their own ideas about what needed to be done. There were also pre-existing tensions among a few early participants who lived in the same apartment buildings.

In the beginning I felt it was my job to try to mediate the conflicts, but I was not particularly skilled in that arena and my efforts to promote harmony were not always successful. Like the many diverse plants in the garden, some are companionable, benefiting one another with proximity, while others struggle when planted nearby. We had to learn the hard way.

A few participants had clearly learned the give and take of communal efforts. Others were less comfortable, or less skilled, in working collectively. I was somewhere in the middle, neither fully confident nor entirely unsure. I was trying to find my way through.

I believed the best path forward was to empower participants so that we all felt ownership of the project. But someone had to hold it all together, especially in those early years when so many were coming and going with varied levels of interest and commitment. I was struggling to find the balance and to encourage all levels of experience, from those who never had planted a seed to others with generations of gardening know how. I could not have anticipated all the challenges.

One summer, a volunteer brought a massive American flag to the garden, displaying it in the center of the garden. It dominated the space, unsettling the Earth-centered ethos I had envisioned. When others also objected to displaying such an enormous flag, we agreed as a garden group that he could affix a much smaller one to his own garden box. Nonetheless, rumors spread in our apartment building that we were "taking down the flag." It was a stark reminder of how quickly misunderstandings can escalate. The tension eventually passed, but it was a reminder of how such symbols can carry weight.

Another conflict came about when one of our new volunteers—ironically, an early naysayer, accepted a large cash donation on-site before we had our accounting system in place. Without consultation, he headed out to buy supplies. When I stepped in to ask if he would wait until we could decide together the best use of the funds, he ignored my request. When I confronted him later, he unleashed a barrage of vulgar invective. I was stunned. He clearly did not respect me or my role as garden manager. It was a position I was trying to define myself. That encounter was a harsh and early hint of conflicts that can arise at the onset of such a challenging community project.

As an organic garden, we discouraged use of soil additives like Miracle-Gro. This restriction caused some disagreements as some of our participants had relied on the product for decades in their own home gardens and were not easily convinced of its detrimental impacts. We had finished compost and a large bag of worm castings to provide rich organic nutrients instead. We all had so much to learn from one another, and there were no real experts among us.

When and where to water also became an issue requiring negotiation. One gardener wanted to use only rainwater on his plants; others felt we should not water anything at certain times of the day. As the summer heated up and the plants began to wilt, I welcomed anyone at any time who offered to help with the task.

Another difficulty came when enthusiastic gardeners would clip and weed in garden plots that had not been well maintained by less experienced or less frequent volunteers. We had to strike a balance between allowing new gardeners to learn through experience and doing the necessary work to maintain the garden's overall appearance and health.

With each new garden season and with every new volunteer, the dynamics changed. I became more relaxed, trusting that the inevitable conflicts and disagreements could be worked out without my intervention. This was not always possible. Some gardeners left due to ongoing personality clashes; others were asked to leave—a rare but necessary decision for maintaining group harmony. Some moved away, others passed away. We have had a constant flow of volunteers through the years adding their unique energy, challenges, and support.

Keeping Accounts

> In nature's economy the currency is not money, it is life.
>
> —Vandana Shiva

Early enthusiasm for creating a neighborhood garden outpaced our organizational structure. As soon as we opened the gates, garden visitors began offering cash donations. It was heartening—but I knew we needed a system in place to manage income and expenses responsibly. I wanted to keep it simple. After all, I came to garden, not to be bogged down with administrative tasks. As the person responsible for assuring compliance with the Use Agreement that I signed with the city, I felt the weight of getting it right. I knew that managing funds in a transparently responsible way was critical to trust.

I was very relieved when a volunteer from the nearby Montford neighborhood, Robert Glenn, stepped up as treasurer. We opened an account with the Self-Help Credit Union in the garden's name and agreed on a simple system to keep track of income and expenditures. By October of our first year, after meeting some early expenses, we had $151.61 left on account. Over the years, after Robert moved on, Linda Wolf became a co-signer on the account, and when she moved away, Cindy Gray agreed, joined recently by David Forbes. The donation boxes on site yield mostly one-dollar bills, sometimes a five, a twenty, and once a passerby handed me a crisp one-hundred-dollar bill.

I have a boxful of income and expense receipts for each month from 2017-2025. It would be an interesting exercise to tally these up to provide an overall account, but I will happily leave that task to anyone who has the inclination. What is clear, however, is that we have managed to develop and maintain this well-tended garden with frugal and careful use of available funds. Most importantly, it is the thousands of hours of in-kind support through the volunteer labor of neighborhood and community elders and others that have sustained our gardens, supplemented with considerable gifts of plants, maintenance materials, and carpentry and gardening skills. Truly a co-creative venture.

That first winter, I learned of a grant opportunity through the Pollination Project—a nonprofit offering micro-grants for social change. I wrote the application, and we soon received a $1,000 check. It bolstered our bank account and lifted our spirits. In addition to The Pollination Project grant, our allies at Bountiful Cities helped with material support for several large projects. Rebecca Chaplin of AARP Western Region, and the Community Garden Partners at NC State A&T also helped. These gifts enabled the purchase of perennial plants, garden soil, sun shelters, tools, lumber and other supplies and materials for garden accessibility.

In those first few years, we convened monthly garden meetings, keeping minutes and sharing them by email. But with participants coming and going, and some staying only a few months, eventually we decided that much of the garden business could best be discussed on-site among those who were reliable and consistently participating in the work.

Chapter Five

Chaos and Crises

> Your garden is a protest for all the ways in which we deny our life by denying other lives. Plant some natives. Be defiantly compassionate.
>
> —Benjamin Vogt

The still-vacant city lots within our neighborhood are considered part of the downtown central business district. They were initially acquired by the city for the purpose of constructing a parking garage. Then a hotel was proposed. When that did not come about, the next proposal was for an office building with an adjoining pocket park. Still, the people held out for a public park, prompting City Council to initiate a public process to guide the future use of the properties.

Asheville Design Center was hired to facilitate the Community Visioning process, and the Haywood Page Master Plan and Conceptual Design project finally kicked off in fall 2019. Garden volunteers attended public meetings where residents were invited to share what components they hoped to see in the design. We supported the work toward a public park and advocated that a community garden be a central feature, realizing that the exact location our current gardens occupied might need to be shifted.

Park Plans Interrupted

The resulting Master Plan for the park, with a $13 million estimated cost, has yet to be funded. The beautiful design remains a concept on its website. We were disappointed to see that the plans approved by the city included only a small, semi-circular section of uniform garden boxes designated as the "community garden."

The likelihood of the park design being funded has had to give way to the significant challenges the city faced with the COVID pandemic in 2020 and with the catastrophe of Hurricane Helene in 2024. And now, Asheville is facing a projected budget gap of $28 million for fiscal year 2026-27.

As I write in 2026, this long-contested public land, still buried in crumbling blacktop and heat-radiating parking lots, stands in stark contrast to the grassroots energized Elder & Sage Community Garden—a product of community-based leadership and effort where a marvelous variety of life thrives, nurturing all who lend their hands to the work. We're doing all that we can to ensure that an authentic community garden— one that reflects the creative spirit of its workers—will be an integral component of any future park design. In the meantime, we carry on, little by little, reclaiming space for life and affirming the rights of nature.

The Global Pandemic

The valerian is in the bud and purple iris blooming.
The virus stalks the people; a sense of dread is looming.

Early in the COVID pandemic the news was filled with reports of deaths among the elderly, particularly those living in nursing homes or congregate housing situations. We at Battery Park quickly realized our vulnerability to the virus. Everyone was nervous about getting too close to anyone else. Already some in our apartment building had succumbed to the spreading infection. Residents of both the Vanderbilt and Battery Park apartments, where most of our volunteer gardeners lived, were offered access to vaccines as soon as they came out. In the meantime, Asheville declared a State of Emergency and limited gatherings on city-owned property to ten people. This posed special challenges for the garden as we could not keep the gates open to visitors without constant monitoring of numbers. We purchased a box of N-95 masks to have on hand for garden volunteers and visitors.

Volunteer Linda Wolf painted new signs for the entrance stating that all our garden volunteers were vaccinated and cautioning visitors to observe social distancing. Another sign advised: "Wear a mask and enter with a happy heart."

In recalling those days, Linda said, "Elder & Sage Community Gardens was my refuge and project during COVID's darkness. We plowed ahead and prevailed and even thrived and the garden became, and is, a haven and relief for many...the Earth always gives us more than we give it."

And Linda gave a lot to the gardens, a legacy of care that continues to brighten the neighborhood long after she moved away.

In early March of 2020, as the pandemic continued, I walked several blocks from my apartment to the French Broad Food Co-op. The streets belonged to the unhoused poor, gathered in clusters here and there or walking alone, burdened with heavy bundles and unmet needs. Most benches were claimed as hard beds of the most vulnerable. One man was fast asleep beside his wheelchair in a doorway of the then vacant 1926-era Flat Iron building. Seventy-one of the building's former tenants, all small local businesses, had been recently evicted after city council approved its sale for conversion to a boutique hotel.[23]

Few lights were visible in the many empty rooms of nearby hotels. All restaurants were closed and the only workers were cleaning up or making take-out deliveries. There was no music from street corner buskers, no pub-cycle shrieks from its cargo of drunken revelers, nor any La Zoom bus jokesters, or Piano Bar truck intrusions. No tourist throngs to navigate along the way, and only the sad stumps of Haywood Street trees and the fat alley rats scurrying about.

When the Buncombe County Public Health Department issued a "Stay Home, Stay Safe" declaration, we closed the garden to outside visitors. Our small group of volunteers were able to access the garden daily to tend our vegetables and herbs. This was a life saver for us, allowing us to get outside our apartments and into the fresh air at a time when so many were confined inside. Perhaps the Corona crisis will give our imperiled planet a little breathing room while commerce slows down, I hoped.

In early spring of the pandemic year, our friends at BeLoved

Community blessed us with several flats of beautiful vegetable starts as part of their "Plants for the People" project. This dedicated community of activists understands the deep inequities that persist living in the second fastest gentrifying city in the country.[24]

"Give elders a gravel parking lot in the middle of downtown and they turn it into a garden oasis," Amy Cantrell posted on BeLoved Asheville's Facebook page that year. "Invest in hotels and tourism, you get emptiness amidst the pandemic...Invest in people and community and they build gardens in the middle of the pain."

During the pandemic lockdown, a news crew from Greeneville, S.C. was in town looking for a story. They noticed Larry Williams at work in the garden and approached him for an interview. "We practice six feet here," he told the reporter, "I've got my mask and my gloves and everything. This garden is healing and a blessing."

Rats and other intruders

> Even in the smallest spaces, the rat finds room to thrive—a
> lesson in making the most of what you have.
> —Yexuechen, ourSpiritAnimal.com

Early in our second summer, a horde of city rats began burrowing into the soft soil of our garden boxes disrupting the vegetable roots and disgusting the gardeners. At dusk we could see them scurrying through the alleyways and scampering across the gravel inside the garden. The bites they took out of our small crop of tomatoes were especially discouraging. Something had to be done.

One of our gardeners asked that the rodents be left unmolested. They were intelligent and sentient beings, not merely vermin to be eradicated, she argued. No doubt these creatures were smart, but they were also destructive. In an effort at compromise, we put a call out for some "Hav' a Heart" live rodent traps. A friend came by with three and we set them out, luring the rats with a healthy dollop of peanut butter. Arturo checked the traps each morning, then drove the captives to the river. Every day, for weeks, more rats found their way into the traps. Occasionally we spotted a hawk diving down from his perch atop the Battery Park Apartments to grasp a fleeing rat and fly away, but the rats were far too numerous for this lone predator to make a significant difference. The rats were invading much of the downtown area and relocating them was not an effective solution.

"It's really a scary idea that, if you have to go out at night, you might step on a rat, or they might scamper over your feet. I still get quivers up my spine when I see one," our neighbor Rachael Bliss was quoted saying in the *Mountain Xpress* in a 2018 story[25] on the city's rat problem.

Asheville's sizable and growing rat population was exacerbated by all the construction disrupting sewage pipes and other rat habitats. With all the underground passages throughout downtown, and the nearby so-called Rat Alley along the length of Wall Street serving as a rear exit to restaurants on Patton Avenue, it was no surprise that the vermin would soon find their way to our gardens.

One morning soon after I opened the gates a garden a visitor called me over. She remarked at how lifelike our decorations seemed. We had ceramic and plastic animals placed here and there in the garden boxes, such as cows and sheep, roosters, and ducks, many gleaned from the bins at the local Goodwill Outlet Store. To my horror, the tourist was pointing to a large rodent hanging by its claws, caught in the plastic netting around a tomato plant. We had tried to protect our just ripening fruit from these marauders. I never expected that one would become entangled and hang there until death.

Discouraged with the problem, Arturo checked the Internet to research nonviolent solutions. "I don't believe in the death penalty for rats," he told me. He found a story about an Australian gardener who affixed a skewer of red-hot peppers in the corners of her garden plot and was successful in repelling the vermin. Arturo sprinkled habanero powder around in the garden boxes, careful not to burn the plants. Soon we noticed fewer rats burrowing there.

But then, we were dealing with intruders of another sort.

Thieves in the Night

> The day is for honest men, the night for thieves.
> —Euripides

One summer morning I was fuming as I opened the back gates to visitors. I had just discovered that our new wagon was gone, and our storage bins rifled through, leaving garden books and seed packets strewn about on the gravel. "How are you doing?" the morning visitor inquired, noticing my agitation. "I'm really mad," I said, telling her of the theft of our wagon.

I described it in as much detail as I could. "I just saw a couple pulling a wagon like that down around Anne Street," she told me. That was just a few blocks away, and I was determined to retrieve our wagon. I called Arturo and we drove around the corner to Haywood Street where we spotted a young couple pulling the wagon along the sidewalk.

I jumped out of the car. "Give it back!" I demanded. The wagon was loaded with sleeping bags and other street survival supplies. My compassion for these internally displaced people, who clearly needed a way to transport their few belongings, was overruled by my anger at the theft. "You're stealing from old people," I admonished. Then I took hold of the handle, emptied the contents at the feet of the startled pair, and walked the wagon back to the garden. Arturo followed in his car. We bought another lock and heavy chain. This wasn't the first garden theft, nor would it be the last.

Each theft from the garden is disheartening. Another time a thief made off with small tools and lovely ceramic planters, again leaving seeds, garden books, and tarps strewn about. But then, in a moment of grace, my neighbor Lori Brinson came by gifting us with garden tools that her great grandmother had used in a wooden box her grandfather made. Oh my. Her thoughtfulness lifted my spirits.

Another time I found that some opportunist had moved a large ceramic pot with a flowering shrub about a block down the sidewalk, only to abandon the heavy load. I enlisted the help of two strong passersby to drag it back to its place in the garden.

Our plantings outside the front gate or along the fence line are vulnerable too, particularly on weekends. We had a crimson dinner-plate dahlia with numerous buds and blossoms growing close to the front fence. It was doing well until a passerby decided to pluck the blossom, uprooting the entire plant. We found it on the gravel the next morning, just in time to get it back in the soil.

Secure storage of tools and other garden necessities has been an ongoing issue from year to year. In early 2025, Salvatore Russo, a native of Sicily, living and farming in nearby Leicester, put in hours of volunteer labor to craft a much-needed tool shed, mostly re-using discarded pallets and scrap wood. A local Sherwin-Williams store donated the paint, and Arturo decorated the outside with bark from fallen trees. We bought another lock and thought we would be secure. But once again thieves jumped the garden fence. This time they threw rotting raw shrimp and produce into a garden bed, broke the lock on our new tool shed, stole two skill saws, a drill, a hammer, screw drivers, and a crowbar, and then attempted to steal from the donation box, though there was nothing there but the penny I left after checking for donations at closing time.

While we do face challenges from night-time opportunists, there are many more people who come forward to help. When the Downtown Improvement District's newly hired "Ambassadors," were touring the neighborhood, I mentioned the recent theft of our tools. A few days later, an "Ambassador" named Willie was pushing his cart past the garden just when I needed a hand to heave a few bags of composted soil over the fence. He said he was happy to help. "We have something for you," he told me, as he put the heavy bags down. Soon he returned with a new tool bag. Inside were battery-operated drills, a saw, work gloves, and other items needed for garden maintenance.

Others also responded generously. Cindy Heil, a friend and volunteer at the Sand Hill Community Garden, sent a check. Then long-time garden allies Marilyn and Larry Shames took up a collection from their downtown neighbors in The Aston Apartments.

Despite the challenges, the garden still blooms and shares its sweet-scented beauty with all who come, even thieves in the night.

Travelers, Trespassers, and Trippers

> I will go where I will go, And I will jettison all dead weight, And I will use these words for kindling, And I will sleep by the garden gate.
>
> —John Darnielle

It seems that every summer a new group of destitute travelers pass through town. We take notice as they pass by the gardens. Some among them are respectful of the space and happy for a little respite from the hot pavement; others seem more interested in checking out the tool storage area or looking for places to easily hop the fence after dark, as many have done over the years. And still others are the lost ones, struggling with mental health or illicit drug use, or just looking for a safe place to lay their heads. But I remain wary.

Today as I write, looking out from my high window I can see a young couple sprawled on the concrete at the edge of the parking lot just outside the garden fence. They are clearly under the influence of some mind-altering substances. I've seen others, often at dusk as I've closed the garden. They move slowly through the alley, like zombies, then pause doubled over from the waist, before taking a few more steps. Eventually they make their way past, perhaps to find refuge for the night in dark corner.

Once I came down to open the garden and had to chase out three young men along with their two dogs who had slept together beneath our sun shelter, littering the ground with their discarded hypodermic needles. Other times we have had to rouse someone sleeping well into the morning at the front gate. We were permissive at first, if they left no trace and had moved on by early morning before we came to open the gardens, but too many times we had to rouse a late sleeper or clean up the debris and occasional excrement left behind.

I've chased a few fence jumpers out of the garden myself. The ones who come at night and linger into the morning. A safe and secure campground accessible by city transit might offer a reasonable alternative to travelers who prefer sleeping outside to city shelter beds, but such community support of the unhoused is not available.

Itinerant travelers and chronically unhoused people are often out and about on the downtown streets. Sometimes a few familiar regulars pass by, and other times the broken ones, loudly proclaiming their grievances to no one in particular. We have made a policy while inside the gardens not to offer money. There are other nearby places where help is available. AHOPE, a day center for the unhoused, is a hub of information and connection with community resources, as is the Haywood Street Congregation and their weekly Downtown Welcome Table. This is a blessing for many who are being chased from pillar to post throughout the city. Our friends at BeLoved Asheville have recently installed a Street Pantry outside Pack Memorial library where many unhoused persons find welcome respite from the streets.

Sometimes we can build relationships with our unhoused neighbors. Sam has been a well-known character around downtown for years. He is a pleasant lanky man, perhaps in his early 40s, who always returns a greeting in his husky and drawling voice, putting down his notebook and pencil to look up and smile. Sam took up residence for many months on the bench under the sycamore tree just outside the garden. He preferred the outdoors to the crowded city shelters. Sam composed music in a small notebook he always had in hand. It seemed he lived a lot in his head, where the music was. He would sometimes sleep in the alley behind the garden in a corner where few people passed. At first, we allowed him to leave his bundle of bedding just over the back fence where we stored tomato cages and unused plant containers, but over time his possessions seemed to multiply, and other bedding bundles began to appear. So, we had to call a halt to that courtesy. Other times he would sleep in the walkway just outside the garden's front gate. Too often I had to sternly let him know that lingering there late in the morning when we came to open the garden was unacceptable. He usually grumbled a bit, as anyone might when roused from a deep sleep. Sam moved to several other places around town, usually in the threshold of a closed or vacant storefront. He would greet me as I passed in his deep voice, a cigarette dangling from his mouth. He said that sometimes he was allowed to play his music on a church organ, but I never had a chance to hear his song. In the months before he moved from Asheville, he looked disheveled and seemed weary. It was evident that street life had taken a toll. I heard from his other friends that he had moved "up North."

As with Sam, not all the unhoused who wander through the neighborhood are thieves, trespassers or addicts. All are economically stressed, and many are obviously mentally unstable. We must set boundaries, even when our compassion pulls us to help. We have tried to set an overall tone and expectation of mutual respect, acknowledging the inherent dignity of all, regardless of social class and circumstance.

Bruce is another familiar presence on Page Avenue. He is a young Black man, large and restless. He usually arrives before dusk, pacing back and forth in front of the garden, his blanket draped over his shoulders, and dragging the ground, before he settles in for the night. When I first noticed him, he was sleeping in the foyer of the vacant building next to the gardens. On hot summer nights he would often be shirtless as he paced the sidewalk or slept sprawled on the threshold. Now that the building has again changed hands and is in process of renovation, Bruce sleeps on the hard bench where Sam once lived. He is a man of few words, slow to respond to a greeting, but never sullen or threatening, except for occasional loud outbursts addressing no visible adversary.

One autumn afternoon I was unearthing sweet potatoes from my garden box near the fence and looked up to see him watching me intently. Before long he had come in through the back gate and was standing close behind me as I worked. "Are those potatoes?" He asked. "Yes, aren't they great? It's my supper tonight, right out of the ground," I said, moving away to the water tap to rinse them off. He soon shuffled out the gate in the worn house slippers he often wears. With the recent hard freeze, I've been worried for him, but as soon as the weather warmed, he was back at the bench. Bruce is but one of the many hundreds of unsheltered and vulnerable people in our wealthy city.

Once I came down to find a large furniture box placed alongside the garden fence. Someone had cut a doorway in the front and inside were blankets and other bedding. This resourceful person had found a way to create temporary shelter with a garden view, a far more private accommodation than the nearby park bench.

"If you sit too long, I'll put you to work," I sometimes say when itinerant visitors linger in the garden. This declaration usually has instant results. Some soon leave, while others gladly offer a helping hand, usually with some small tasks I have suggested, like moving a heavy pot or lifting a bag of soil. I believe such reciprocity is important in developing a relationship of mutuality.

Moe is another familiar visitor to the neighborhood. I've had a passing acquaintance with him for decades. Sometimes I encounter him on the city bus, or on a bench here and there around town. He has lived in Asheville for a long time, one of the few local Black folks that frequent downtown. Moe passes by the garden often, always asking: "What can I help you with today?" We have moved heavy pots, shoveled soil, and rearranged garden furniture. "I'm an old farm boy," he told me. "I know how to work." He's a good listener too. And we have had many interesting conversations about the state of the country and the world. "What kind of trouble are you getting into now?" he often asks. Once he suggested that the city let me have access to the lot for a garden just to keep me busy and out of trouble. It certainly has kept me busy,

Where is a Bear to Go?

With all the development and habitat encroachment, our urban black bears are now competing for space with the outpriced and internally displaced poor. A juvenile black bear strolled through the garden one fall afternoon in 2024. It startled me with its powerful presence. The wild visitor wandered around a bit sniffing the plants then ambled out the back gate. He had been spotted by a throng of tourists who pursued him down the alley, cell-phone cameras in hand.

A once-wooded area adjacent to the Interstate and visible from the back of our apartment building had been used by an unhoused person as a campsite; later it became a den for a black bear who wandered around in the early morning alarming my elderly neighbors who were out walking their dogs. "We have bears that den up along that stretch of the interstate that goes right through downtown. So, it's not uncommon to see bears in that area,"[26] according to Ashley Hobbs of the N.C. Wildlife Resources Commission.

Those few trees and shrubs and the adjacent surface parking lot are gone now, and a new, high-priced, bland and boring condominium is rising there. I miss that bear.

Hurricane Helene's Havoc

> Water Is Life. Listen: as water drips and whispers, babbles
> and swirls and rushes with hurricane-force winds: screaming.
> What is water saying?
> —Gretchen Ernster Henderson

In the fall of 2024 Hurricane Helene unleashed her fury in these mountains. Although it had been downgraded to a Tropical Storm, Helene arrived with winds on nearby Mount Mitchell clocked at eighty miles per hour. These were traumatic times when floodwaters swept away people, roads, homes, and businesses throughout the area. One hundred-eight people died in North Carolina, and eighteen in Tennessee were lost in the deluge. Downtown Asheville was not as tragically impacted as outlying areas, though we lost cell communications, internet, and water. The reservoir that supplies Asheville's drinking water filled with mud and debris from landslides. Water lines were broken. The city provided drinking water from tankers, and ample quantities of bottled drinking water were made available throughout the 52-day outage.

Local volunteers, known as the Flush Brigade, filled water barrels in our gardens and crowdsourced buckets and trucks to deliver non-potable water to flush toilets around town, helping to avoid a sanitation disaster. We were hauling water again, this time up from the garden and into our apartments, making the trek across the street and up the elevators.

It was a grim time all around, particularly outside the downtown area. Luckily, even though the high winds and heavy rains ripped apart our sun shelters and the garden furniture and decorations were blown about, the damage to plants and garden beds was minimal.

Our friends at BeLoved Community were on the ground immediately to help. They had limited cell service and a network of allies developed through their years of community action. "We knew it was the moment we had to figure our way out because nobody was coming to rescue us," Ponkho told interviewer Allison Sherman in her 2025 article, "Helene Heroes — Ponkho Bermejo, BeLoved Asheville."[27]

After the storms, Arturo and fellow workers Franco and Salvatore gathered downed limbs and logs to repurpose in the garden. We filled the hollow centers with soil and plants to commemorate the loss while bringing forth new life in the shell of the old. An estimated forty percent of existing trees were lost or damaged in the county. An astounding number of fallen trees and debris were piled throughout the city. Many little birds were left out in the cold. Arturo found a fallen finch with a broken wing. He tenderly nurtured it for days, until sadly it left us before we could hear its song. He buried it in the garden beside a beautiful rose bush.

It wasn't just Asheville that suffered the wrath of Hurricane Helene. The entire Flowering Bridge, planted along a century-old span over the Rocky Broad River in the nearby town of Lake Lure, was demolished by flood waters. The damage there was so extensive that the work of many years was washed away in one night. A harsh lesson in impermanence.

Chapter Six

Collaborating and Connecting

On a typical summer day, thousands of tourists move through downtown. Many stop in the gardens and show their appreciation with donations that help sustain our work. This generous show of appreciation has provided a comfortable balance in our Self-Help Credit Union Account. As I write now, after making the final deposit of the 2025 season, we have $1,595.67 on hand to help with garden expenses in our upcoming 10th season.

"Front Porch" Conversations

> This is a wonderful place for enjoying life while striking up conversations with the locals who live nearby or occasionally with the more adventurous tourist that has stepped off the well-used trail for a slice of natural reality and local beauty.
>
> —Scott Owen

Our sun shelters have served much like a neighborhood front porch. We greet all who pass through and often share local stories, garden lore, and information on nearby points of interest. We have had many rich conversations. We enjoy these interactions. Many visitors tell us of the community gardens they tend at home or in their neighborhoods and are delighted to find familiar plants growing in our gardens. Tourists often share information about the benefits and uses of our culinary and medicinal plants and appreciate the comfortable, child-friendly atmosphere in the non-commercial authentically Asheville setting.

Sometimes we can guess just where the Tourist Development Authority has been advertising from the hometowns of garden visitors. The TDA uses most of its vast funds accrued from hotel room taxes to advertise Asheville throughout the country and world, but not enough is used to mitigate the impacts on residents and infrastructure. More than thirteen million tourists visited Asheville last year. As one recent study has warned, such a volume of out-of-town visitors can "lead to overcrowded public spaces, increased traffic congestion, and elevated demand for essential services. Residents may find their neighborhoods transformed, with a focus on catering to visitors rather than supporting local lifestyles."[28] This is certainly evident in our downtown Asheville neighborhoods.

We take every opportunity to add to our garden. When Battery Park Apartments were undergoing renovations to the front porch, we learned that management was getting rid of two vintage concrete tables and benches. If we wanted to save them, we had to act fast. They gave us three days. Old friend Jim Brown alerted his son Matt, and together they managed to move the very heavy tables across the street and into our gardens. Scott gifted us with a wooden picnic table, so we had ample space to accommodate our lunch-time guests. We are always happy to see local service workers and nearby residents come into the garden, many seeking a comfortable place to rest or to read in the shade of a tree. Some bring their lunch; others just amble through for a breath of fresh air.

One rainy March morning I was out in the garden checking the sun shelters, as they sometimes collect water and stress the frame. As I opened the gates, a large group of tourists from Minnesota, gardeners all, were waiting outside. I was happy to share with them our efforts to hold the ground and keep the space for a diversity of green and growing life amidst the crumbling asphalt surrounding us. They were eager to see what plants were still thriving in our less harsh winter climate.

One afternoon, shortly after Hurricane Helene, I was lamenting the loss of yet another pop-up sun shelter when I noticed a man taking photos over the back fence. I mentioned our loss. He said he worked with The Preservation Society of Asheville, and that they just might have a replacement for us. A few days later he had returned with a used but still functional shelter. Another time, in midsummer, I welcomed a large group of master gardeners in town for the 2024 National Symposium of the Perennial Plant Association. Though we were not listed on their official tour, it was nice to hear compliments from some of the best!

Sometimes local musicians drop by adding to the garden ambiance. Hafid Lalaoui, a native of Morocco now living in the Vanderbilt Apartments, has graced our gardens many times with the exotic sounds of his violin. Sometimes he practices a bit in the gardens before joining other buskers on downtown streets.

Intergenerational Energizing

Our community garden is well situated to provide opportunities for intergenerational education and sharing. Linda often brought her granddaughter Lovella along with her when she came to volunteer. Together they painted river rocks and decorated the garden boxes. Since they moved away, we have missed their lively and helpful spirits.

Larry Holloway's great niece E'niyah eagerly helps him with garden chores when she is in town. E'niyah is curious and talkative as she moves about the garden, and she loves to offer tours to visitors, pointing out her favorite blossoms. This year they planted squash together. When she saw how quickly the seeds sprouted and grew, her excitement was contagious. They make a good team, watering the planters in the summer and gathering up the fallen leaves when autumn arrives. Larry's t-shirt, "Busy Doing Nothing," belies his helpful manner. He is also an amateur artist. One year he brought a new canvas to the garden, and we proudly displayed his creation. It was a back-handed compliment, we joked, when his artwork was among the items stolen by a fence-jumping crook.

Many times, as families pass by the garden, the children plead with their parents to come inside. Arturo devised an uncomplicated way to entertain the little ones. We reward their curiosity with a chance to find and keep a tiny dinosaur hidden among the planters. Before long they are off and running, inspecting all the planters and in the process, they notice the vegetables and herbs growing there. We also have small watering cans available and invite the children to give the plants a drink.

Max Gunther, who works nearby at Kimmel & Associates, sometimes brings his two daughters Zoe and Corina to the garden. They help tend two planters of flowers and tomatoes. Max always has an encouraging word as he passes by and is always willing to help, especially with heavy lifting. It is always uplifting when children add their excited energy to the gardens, and we do our best to make them feel welcome.

Connecting across Borders

Toward the end of October of our first year, Ponkho of BeLoved Community came by with a large painting of La Calavera Catrina, depicting the head of a skeletal woman in a large, plumed hat mocking the living. The image was inspired by Guadalupe Posado, a graphic artist from Ponkho's hometown, Aguascalientes, Mexico. The image is associated with Dia de los Muertos, the day of the dead, and has become an icon of Mexican identity.

"People like to celebrate our cultural traditions and enjoy our food," Ponkho told me, "But they don't really want to know the truth about our struggles." When we fail to recognize the inherent dignity of immigrants, regardless of documented status, we lose the opportunity to learn from diverse cultures and the traditional knowledge they carry.

Our neighbor chef Hector Diaz, a Puerto Rico native whose Asheville restaurants are known for their Caribbean-Latin cuisine, joined us in the gardens in 2025 to plant a fresh bed of culinary herbs. He brought his sons with him to help sow the seeds and was happy to see the nutrient-rich purslane (*Portulaca oleracea*) and pungent *epazote* already growing nearby. The garden nourishes more than soil; it feeds creativity and connection and offers many surprises.

In the fall of 2024, Arturo led a garden tour with the Spanish conversation class from Pack Memorial Library, pointing out the Spanish names and uses of many of the plants. These events aren't just about gardening, they're about cultivating relationships, sharing wisdom, and celebrating the power of community. It would be wonderful if we could label all the plants bilingually and cultivate more cross-culture sharing. As always seems to be the case, we have many more suggestions and ideas than volunteer capacity.

I am mindful of the struggles of immigrants each time I see a monarch butterfly alighting on a native milkweed plant or sipping the nectar of a purple coneflower blossom before the long and brave flight to Mexico.

Our international visitors feel welcome among our bilingual and multicultural volunteers. One bright fall afternoon Arturo's friend, the pizza chef at the nearby Modesto restaurant, stopped by the garden on his way to work. I was busy painting a weather-worn tabletop and caught only snippets of their lively Spanish conversation as they walked around the garden, pausing to comment on several of the herbs we cultivate. "He is an indigenous Mayan, and knows a lot about the plants," Arturo told me. Maybe next season we can offer another bilingual tour.

One afternoon a botany professor from Haiti visited the gardens while touring Asheville. Arturo was weeding in his box when the man approached. "Oh, you have datura. Did you plant it?" Arturo told him that he had not, that it might have arrived along with the manure. "Ah, but datura chose you," the professor replied with a smile. He then recounted some of the many sacred and ritual uses in indigenous cultures of this powerful psychotropic said to induce intense visions.

Datura (*Datura stramonium*), a native of Central America, is a prolific, self-seeding immigrant. Its night blooming solitary white blossom with violet hues is a beauty to behold. Datura first appeared in Arturo's garden box, alongside his peppers and tomatoes, both also in the nightshade family of plants. Now that we are aware of its dangers to the unwary and uninitiated, we uproot this fascinating plant, with apologies. In more local lore, English soldiers sent to Jamestown, Virginia, to suppress a settler's rebellion spent eleven days in a state of delirium after consuming datura, hence its common name, "jimson weed."

Visitors from India notice the tulsi basil (*Ocimum sanctum*), with its heavenly scent. This herb is native to India where it is held in high esteem. Tulsi is believed to cleanse the environment, bring positive energy, and promote well-being. I use leaves and flowering tops for tinctures and tea throughout the winter. It is considered a "superior herb" because of its many spiritual and nutritional benefits.

Other Asian visitors admire the perilla (*Perilla frutescens,*) a prolific, and nutritious deep purple herb in the mint family that is used in Korean cooking and valued for its healing and nutritional qualities.

Another quite different immigrant resident of our herb garden is rue (*Ruta graveolens*), known as "ruda" in Spanish. Rue, a bitter herb, is said to have protective power to purify spaces, to break curses and hexes, and to attract love and good luck. Its diminutive yellow blooms also attract butterflies. I have yet to give its culinary uses a try, but I am happy for any good luck it might bring.

The pungent herb *epazote* (*Dysphania ambrosioides*) volunteered from seed that likely arrived with the composted soil. The plant has been in culinary and medicinal use as far back as Aztec times. It is a digestive aid used in many Mexican and Latin American dishes, and a healing tea. Epazote returns year after year, rising here and there throughout the garden. Last fall after I let one plant go to seed it grew nearly four feet tall with thousands of seeds along the stem. We may have quite a crop of this aromatic herb next season.

The persistent and much maligned princess tree (*Paulownia tomentosa*), an immigrant from China, pushed up through the gravel with an astounding strength and rapid growth. Visitors from out of the region often inquire about this remarkable tree that is often seen chopped and maimed along the roadsides and wastelands of the inner city. These trees are well suited on our "temporary use" urban gravel lot, spreading their huge leaves to provide shade and absorbing much of the poison CO_2 from the thousands of cars passing by on local streets and the nearby Interstate highway. The remarkably efficient carbon sequestration of this stunning immigrant is an asset in these times of escalating climate disasters. The strong yet lightweight hardwood, like that of basswood and alder, is cultivated in Germany for crafting guitars, saving vulnerable tree species like mahogany.

Culinary Gatherings

The Elder & Sage Community Gardens are a powerful force for connection, sustainability, and healing. We work cooperatively hosting and participating in social and informational gatherings that help contribute to a strong network of community gardeners.

In the summer of 2022, Arturo and I were invited to participate in a panel as part of the Chow Chow food festival and culinary event series, a gathering celebrating the unique foodways of Southern Appalachia. The panel included representatives from other local community gardens, with the intent of fostering dialogue about issues including racial justice, climate change, and food justice.

We also participated for several years in Bountiful Cities Urban Garden Tour and Tasting, part of a citywide celebration of urban agriculture. Many community gardens were selected to pair up with a local food vendor or restaurant to offer tasty bites prepared by local chefs. Our garden volunteer Linda Wolf was an immense help as liaison for these events, setting up the garden and greeting the many visitors.

In 2023 the award-winning Chai Pani restaurant provided some of its Indian street food in our gardens as one stop on the Urban Garden Tour and Tasting. That was a particular honor as earlier that year, Meherwan Irani, chef, and co-founder of Chai Pani, was invited to prepare the State Department Luncheon in Washington, D.C., in honor of Prime Minister Narendra Modi of India and his Indian delegation.

On two other occasions Arturo, an avid chef, was invited to highlight his culinary gifts. He shared recipes he learned from his mother in Ecuador using herbs and vegetables grown in our gardens. Salvatore led the visitors on a tour of the gardens, pointing out culinary use of many of the herbs we grow.

Workdays

During spring and fall we have a lot of clean up, paint up, fix up to keep us busy. Sometimes we call on the wider community to help, advertising our needs in the Bountiful Cities network newsletter. Organizing a group of volunteers for a workday takes additional time and planning beyond the day-to-day work of tending to the plants. But working side by side naturally sparks conversation and camaraderie and helps to strengthen community.

When I need help, I often call upon passing tourists. I keep my eye out for strong young people to lend a hand moving a heavy planter, emptying a wheelbarrow of clippings, uprooting a winter-killed shrub, or winding up a hose. They seldom decline the request and leave having done their good deed for the day. I reward them with effusive thanks and a clipping of a fragrant herb, like rosemary, chocolate mint, or thyme.

Isa Whitaker, a garden network coordinator with Bountiful Cities, has always been a willing helper when we do organize a workday. And we can always count on Joe Fioccola. Joe showed us a labor-saving technique to move our large planters across the gravel that he called "building the railroad." He laid the metal poles we kept from our first sun shelter on the gravel and slid the large containers along the "rails." When I ran into Joe at the WNC Seed Swap event this year, I once again thanked him for sharing this valuable trick, especially helpful after our hand truck was stolen from the garden.

For two spring seasons a group of University of Tennessee students on spring break offered an afternoon of high energy help. It was the first Asheville visit for most. They repaired and painted garden boxes, laid stone borders, hauled soil, and added a vibrant inter-generational vibe.

Sometimes the workload feels uneven, with some chores left undone longer than ideal, such as cleaning and sharpening of tools, saving and managing seeds, cleaning and storing garden pots, emptying the trash cans, repairing garden boxes, and hauling away debris. But little by little and enlisting the help of visitors and younger garden friends, we keep going.

When I first meet new gardeners, I am quick to admit I am no expert and appreciate learning from everyone who comes. I am grateful to all who help for an hour, a day, a season, flitting through like the monarch that rests for a time on the milkweed, or returning every summer like the pair of American goldfinches that delight us with their presence.

Marti and Don Marfia, from Mars Hill, N.C., volunteered in 2023 and 2024. Marti planted perennial flowers and a succulent garden that she built with stacked cinder blocks and brought a generous heart and whimsical ornaments to decorate the shared areas. Don spent days taking apart and rebuilding the weathered worktables and storage area at the back of the garden.

Salvatore set to work rebuilding and redesigning some deteriorating garden beds. He also brought new varieties of plants from his home garden. He introduced us to *fenugreek* (*Trigonella foenum-graecum*), a Mediterranean herb with seeds helpful in lowering blood sugar levels in diabetics. He also planted *gotu kola* (*Centella asiatica*), another healing herb, and the diminutive evergreen *santolina* (*Santolina chamaecyparissus*) that has nicely filled out the planter with its fragrant beauty. One afternoon he treated us all to the sweet fruit of the American pawpaw (*Asimina triloba*) from his home gardens, and a seedling we can nourish for the future.

Franco Masci from Tuscany is another cook who found his way to the gardens in 2025, and was soon at work adding his special touch and love of gardens. He is a prolific author and sculptor, who also works in mosaic and murals. His distinctive sculptures and his eye for color and texture combinations have added a cosmopolitan flair to the gardens.

"I'm a student of life," Franco says. "My relationship with the natural world is a direct communication with God."

Diane Ashworth and Cheryl Wegner, both in their 80s and with a good amount of gardening experience, joined us this past season. Both were happy to find a garden across from the Battery Park Apartments when they moved here. This year Cheryl helped keep the gates open to visitors and cleaned all our hand tools, a task that had long awaited a willing volunteer. Diane has planted a variety of vegetables and is optimistic about our garden's long-term survival. She plans to start some asparagus next year, a crop that takes three years to reach harvest.

Cindy Gray has been with us since our early days. She is usually the first to plant tomatoes and gets a jump on the season. This year she planted wildflowers including cosmos and Mexican sunflowers that bloomed well into the fall. Cindy has moved from the Battery Park Apartments but remains a valuable ally and contributor and her garden bed is abuzz with bees.

Anna Gordon joined us in 2025. She works downtown with the NOAA's Center for Environmental Information (NCEI) as a Climate Service Liaison. She has a degree in Environmental Science and Sustainability. But in the gardens, she helps plant and water the collards and kale, shares her hot peppers, and encourages us with her cooperative spirit.

David Forbes, an investigative journalist and editor of the local digital publication *The Asheville Blade*, lives nearby. She has helped keep the gates open early evenings, greets visitors, checks the donation boxes, and grows onions, peppers, tomatoes, and other vegetables. David has kept me in touch with local politics and the escalating challenges faced by the local trans community.

Pack Memorial Library staff have also been helpful contributors. Jen Waite, now the Branch Manager at the Fairview Library, initiated the Poetry for Passersby kiosk that her husband Scott built and installed. Carissa Pfeiffer, a Special Collections librarian, has been selecting and posting new poetry. She keeps our free library stocked with a thoughtful collection of children's books. Drea Dreiling, who facilitates the Asheville Spanish Club at the library organized a library gardening club and together they built and planted a new bed with tomatoes, basil, peppers, and cucumbers. Each of these librarians keeps quite busy with their professional work, but we have benefited greatly from their voluntary solidarity and support whenever they find the time.

Chapter Seven

Gardening through the Seasons

> …Golden, calm as the dawn, the spring's first dandelion
> shows its trustful face.
>
> —Walt Whitman

Spring Awakenings

As the season warms, the crocus, daffodils, narcissus, and tulips begin to push through the soil at the front fence. Inside the garden boxes the purple dead nettle (*Lamium purpureum*), chickweed (*Stellaria media*) and sweet violets peek through the leaf mulch. Each offers early nutrition and beauty. The golden dandelions (*Taraxacum officinale*) pop up here and there from the gravel. I do my best to protect this early source of nectar from enthusiastic weeders.

We also must keep a watchful eye out for the perennial herbs hidden below the soil in many of the raised beds. The clary sage (*Salvia sclarea*) shows its magnificent promise in a rosette of early leaves, and the red stalks and robust leaves of the rhubarb (*Rheum rhabarbarum*) will be well up in their plot. Soon the valerian, sage, and thyme will show themselves, and the native wisteria (*Wisteria frutescens*), a gift from dear friend and gardener Debralee Williams, will come into bud along the fence.

We try to have the gates open to visitors in early April when the lilac opens in sweet bloom. So as soon as the weather permits, we are busy repairing boxes and doing other early chores. Early spring is when we determine which garden spaces will be available to newcomers, and which containers will continue to be maintained by returning gardeners. We always have many aspiring gardeners come forward when drab winter lets go of its chilly grip, but not all who begin will follow through with their early intent. I've learned to accept whatever level of participation and commitment is offered, trusting that the garden itself will draw in the right helpers when needed.

Our robust rosemary shrub did not survive one harsh winter. It was rooted deep into the gravel and seemed impossible to pull out. While I was struggling with the task, a group of Georgia Tech graduates on spring break came through. I saw my opportunity. Like the legendary sword, placed by the Goddess of Creation herself and embedded within a rock, our rosemary roots could only be pulled out by a hero. I asked the young men: "Who among you is strong enough?" They rose to the challenge, and one after the other picked up the shovel and dug into the gravel until the stubborn, freeze-killed roots let go. Heroes all, and the best kind of tourists!

Summer Sizzle

> Gardens are not made by singing "Oh, how beautiful,"
> and sitting in the shade.
> —Rudyard Kipling

In mid-summer when it is muggy and hot, the heat from the surrounding blacktop parking lots and the surface gravel magnifies the harshness of the angry sun. This is the season when the heirloom tomatoes are coming on strong, all sizes and shapes, turning bright red or golden yellow and my favorite, the dark Cherokee purple. Other perennials are coming into their fullness with colors, scents and textures that delight the eye and lift our spirits. We need to be home from the garden by 11 a.m. and not back out until around 6 p.m. to avoid the dizzying, dehydrating solar danger. We keep bottled water on hand and remind each other often to stay hydrated as we work. Ah, but the beauty, the beauty keeps me coming back despite the heat.

Joe Pye weed (*Eutrochium purpureum*) is showing its lovely mauve blooms, content enough in its large container. Ours is a much smaller version of the tall beauties that live along the country roads. This pollinator-friendly native attracts local bees, butterflies and songbirds that tenaciously traverse the wastelands of surface parking and busy streets surrounding our urban garden.

The cut-leaf coneflower (*Rudbeckia laciniata*), also known as *sochan*, is a traditional Cherokee food and nutritious relative of the sunflower. It has grown to a towering height, its yellow blossoms waving in the humid air and obscuring the view of the civic center across the parking lot. Harrah's Cherokee Center now has naming rights for the venue. In our gardens, the sochan is a living reminder of the Cherokee people who nurtured these lands for centuries.

Rosemary (*Salvia rosmarinus*) thrives in our large herb garden, though sometimes we have to replant after a killing freeze. We appreciate it for its culinary and medicinal uses, as well as its pungent scent and the lovely blue blossoms. Fennel (*Foeniculum vulgare*) returns each year with its anise-flavored seeds, as do the healing allies valerian (*Valeriana officinalis*), and echinacea (*Echinacea purpurea*). Catmint, of which there are many species in the nepeta genus of the mint family *lamiaceae*, and the sometimes-confused catnip (*Nepeta cataria*) also have found a space to grow. Another favorite is the hybrid chocolate mint. It would love to have the run of the garden. We freely offer it to visitors who are delighted with its scent. We have several varieties of thyme (*Thymus vulgaris*) that are free for the picking. The pineapple sage (*Salvia elegans*) is blooming brightly, and the elderberry (*Sambucus nigra*) will soon have fruit.

Our prize fig bush escaped its large container last year, its thick root pushing out through a crack and reaching deep into the gravel. Salvatore replanted it where it has more room to grow. This season it was full of fruit. Arturo makes a delicious fig jam with a recipe learned from his mother, and he shares it with appreciative neighbors.

Nearby the lovely Appalachian mountain mint (*Pycnanthemum flexuosum*) is blooming. Its pale green flower clusters are distinctive and attract many pollinators. It makes a great cold-water infusion along with tulsi basil for hydrating on these sweltering afternoons.

Each summer we also harvest blue vervain (*Verbena hastata*) and lemon balm (*Melissa officinalis*) The infusion brings on sweet sleep after a day's work. Volunteer trees that sprouted from beneath the gravel and along the fence line grace us with shade, shelter the songbirds and catch the summer breezes. Young trees, a hybrid relative of the sycamore, have grown tall along the fenceline, providing cooling shade from the asphalt heat desert surrounding the garden.

The bright orange dark-spotted tiger lily (*Lilium lancifolium*), an Asian beauty that gardener Tom Nanney planted, blooms mid-summer with grand style. They are long-lasting and drought tolerant and catch the eye of everyone coming through.

Our milk thistle (*Silybum marianum*) boldly rises with her prickly strength returning year after year from the earth-smothering gravel to reach for the sun. I protect her from garden volunteers who see only a weed. For me, it's a summer delight when the pale purple blossoms emerge. Nectar and pollen from the thistle support diverse pollinators so even this prickly plant is welcome.

The native pollinator wild quinine (*Parthenium integrifolium*), with white, button-like blossoms, has a special space in our gardens. It was the primary ingredient in E. W. Grove's Tasteless Chill Tonic. Tour guides who pass the garden tell how Grove made his fortune selling his quinine remedy. It outpaced Coca-Cola in sales, and its profits funded both the Grove Arcade across from the garden and the Grove Park Inn, built in 1909 on the western-facing slope of Sunset Mountain, and visible from my apartment. Wild quinine became a substitute for the bark of the South American cinchona tree used to treat malaria. Arturo delights in telling the story of how quinine may have saved the life of President Teddy Roosevelt on his African expeditions.

Fall Release

> Then summer fades and passes and October comes. We'll smell smoke then, and feel an unexpected sharpness, a thrill of nervousness, swift elation, a sense of sadness and departure.
>
> —Thomas Wolfe

In September the dusk sky above the garden fills with the return of the chimney swifts (*Chaetura pelagica*). They swirl about in the thousands before spiraling down into nearby chimneys where they roost for the night.

Even as late as October, the Eastern monarchs (*Danaus plexippus L.*) are still fluttering about the remaining goldenrod and aster blossoms feeding on the nectar as they prepare for a remarkable 1,500-mile journey to Mexico. I marvel at their beauty and fragility traversing so much asphalt and concrete to visit our gardens. This past year I didn't find any eggs on the milkweed and saw very few monarchs with their distinctive orange and black patterned wings. Sadly, habitat loss and climate change are major contributors to their significant population decline.

The white wood aster (*Eurybia divaricate*) is blooming all along the front fence with clusters of tiny starry flowers and heart shaped leaves. It is prolific in the Appalachians where one of its common names is "Farewell Summer." It's a favorite of bees and butterflies and a food source for birds. The late purple asters and goldenrod are also in bloom.

On these beautiful fall afternoons, when the sky is endless blue, I spend as much time as possible in the garden. It is a melancholy time of year. Dusk comes early and a crisp coolness brings relief from summer's heat. In the high branches the rhythmic song of the Southeastern dusk singing cicada (*Megatibicen figuratus*) foretells summer's end.

Last fall a multi-colored parakeet took up residence in the branches of a garden tree. Arturo named her "Condorito," after a favorite childhood comic character. She was a delightful visitor for a short time and moved on before the cold winds began to blow.

The sweet gum tree (*Liquidambar styraciflua*) at the front fence shows its colors slowly: A bit of bronze brightens the upper branches, and the spiky gumballs decorate the limbs. The robust princess trees (*Paulownia tomentosa*), that pushed through the gravel and offered shade all summer, drop their leaves first. Deep brown edges frame their large heart-shaped leaves, while the veins remain bright green—a stunning pattern of farewell.

We must balance our garden clean up with the need to leave winter nesting places for native bees and other beneficial insects. The leaves provide a layer of protection from the cold. But we also need to be mindful that the garden appears well tended, situated as we are in a busy tourist area. We have designated a back section of the gardens for a leaf pile and will use them later to help build the soil in our vegetable plots.

As the plants go to seed, we gather what we can of the remaining fruits—the tomatoes, some not yet ripened; cucumbers and squash, some long hidden beneath the vines that nourished them. The basil is still thriving, and red peppers and green peppers are clinging to the stems. Collards and kale and chard are happy with the cooler temperatures and will provide good eating for months to come. The muscadine grapes (*Vitis rotundifolia*) have ripened, hiding in the foliage along the fence. They offer a tartly sweet flavor we look forward to each year.

One November, our friends at BeLoved Community brought Thanksgiving dinner and loving hearts to the neighborhood. They parked their food truck outside the garden gates and across from the Battery Park Apartments. We are grateful for their good work and deep compassion. After Hurricane Helene, they soon turned their energy and resources to help repair and build homes for many devastated by the winds and floods of that catastrophe.

Winter Rest

> But there are roses, there are still roses. In the damp and
> the cold, on a bush that looks done, there's a wide-open
> rose, still. Look at the colour of it.
> —Ali Smith

We take a break from the garden in early winter for much-needed rest. From November through February the weather is usually cold, with intermittent days of sunshine and warmth. Sometimes snowfall blankets the garden. Some of our perennials persist, others do not make it. One year we purchased a portable greenhouse to winter over some of our favorites, but winds, ice, and snow stressed the structure, and we had to let it go. During several winters in earlier years, we were out at first frost with sheets and other protective materials trying to ward off damage, but that too became an onerous and not so successful labor. Learning to let go is a valuable lesson.

The garden feels barren mid-winter, except for the evergreen trees and rosemary shrubs that hold the space. Yet life persists. Some plants even thrive in the cold. Our collards taste sweeter after frost, and the chard and kale and parsley carry on.

As I write in this bleak and unusually cold early December, the brick building adjacent to the gardens has changed hands again and is under renovation by new owners. Thankfully, the construction crew waited until November to erect scaffolding inside the garden and alongside the wall. Much is in disarray and I'm eager to put things back in order.

If I sit at my desk too long the glow of the screen tires my eyes, and I need to be up and moving. On less frigid days I would be out to the garden for a few hours of physical labor, clearing debris along the fence-line, harvesting winter greens, or gathering the fallen leaves into a pile for overwintering insects. This helps clear mental fatigue. Instead, I can walk out to our top-floor porch and look out over the neighborhood, dominated by the drab grey parking lots, and brightened with the Christmas lights twinkling in the bare branches. And beneath the chilled soil in our garden boxes the roots of so many perennial beauties are resting and gathering strength to rise again, and so must I.

Our late January winter storms this year brought ice and snow, high winds and impassable streets. The frigid temperatures were in the single digits for days. The neighborhood fell quiet and the drab grey urban desert of parking lots was softened by a layer of snow. I worried about the unhoused among us, and the tiny birds still hiding in the bushes. Only time will tell how many of our garden perennials have survived.

In early February I look for the Lenten rose (*Helleborus orientalis*) to come into bud. By late March the purple crocus (*Crocus vernus*), diminutive kin of the iris, will be blooming, and valerian (*Valeriana officinalis*), Clary sage (*Salvia sclarea*), and rhubarb (*Rheum rhabarbarum*) will push up through the soil. Soon, and very soon.

Chapter Eight
Moving Forward

We are adults born into these troubled times and we are being called upon to step up and meet life and nature where it's at."
—Sarah Wilson, TEDxSydney
"How to Respond to Societal Collapse."

Many people are coming to realize how important it is to our collective well-being to connect with neighbors in projects for the common good. Community gardens can restore some of the healing beauty so woefully absent in our car-centric city. All community gardens are unique, reflecting the strengths and needs of the neighborhood where they are cultivated, and the vision of those who come forward to do the work.

So many have passed through our garden gates over these past nine years. The community of life nurtured here in such a busy urban environment has gladdened the heart of many and provided respite, if only briefly, from the heaviness of the world. Everyone who comes makes a unique contribution that has enhanced this sacred public space. We often hear passing tourists express surprise and delight when they come upon our oasis of green.

"You are changing the world," activist musician David LaMotte writes, by "participating where you show up, in whatever big or small way that place and that moment demand."[29]

Since the beginning, the uncertainty of our year-to-year use agreement has been an ongoing tension. Perennials take time to establish and grow, so do communities of volunteers. For several years now Bountiful Cities has been the primary liaison between our garden group and the City of Asheville. I was relieved to relinquish that role. Even so, our garden group has continued as on-site managers with autonomy within the terms of the Use Agreement and have kept the gardens alive and vibrant for nine years.

As I write today, in the fall of 2025, we have just learned of our renewed one-year contract with the city for use of the lot. Next year we will begin our 10th gardening season. We work hard to keep this project going. Our core volunteers spend two to three hours daily on general maintenance. Others come to help keep the gates open and greet our many visitors.

My goal is to continue with volunteer garden management through our 10th season. By then, I trust that funds and interest will be sufficient to provide some compensation to a few regular volunteers who will commit to the day-to-day responsibilities to keep the gardens thriving and the gates open to visitors.

I was surprised to learn recently that the 2025 average wage for a community garden manager is about $25 hourly. We all believe it would be a great investment for our garden and the city of Asheville to ensure this urban oasis can be sustained.

The most tangible measure of success is the joy we see on the faces of our gardeners, brightened by the sight of a familiar flower, and pleased with the taste of a carefully nurtured tomato, the earthy smell of freshly dug potatoes, or the sweetness of a fresh strawberry. The return of so many birds and butterflies and other beneficial insects is another sign of our success. We have learned, as we have gone along, how to work together to create and maintain an urban garden.

In the gardens we observe the truth of the natural cycle of change and transition that is the essence of life. The answer to what really matters and how we choose to live in these stressful times can be found in proximity to and communing with the natural world.

As the poet Stephen Wing has written, "Any place is powerful where we choose to stand and give our lives to the Earth."[30]

Who knows how much longer our garden will exist. The professional park design that the city approved is elegant, and it would add grace and beauty to replace the surface parking that blights the neighborhood. Sadly, our existing grassroots-designed gardens were not part of the plan.

So, we do the work before us, planting and tending and loving the beauty that we have cultivated over the years. All these perennial plant stakeholders that have nourished and delighted so many should certainly become an integral component of a larger park and civic plaza. The presence of neighborhood community gardeners on site would enliven a public park with a unique local spirit and commitment to care.

As I consider just how to close this story, my heart is heavy with our nation and the world in chaos and upheaval. I can only hope that the harsh winds of tyranny will stimulate in us the deep changes needed to rise courageously from the darkness, much like the perennial seeds that require prolonged cold before germination. As we nurture respect for the living earth, we elders have a vital part to play. If we listen, if we act, if we summon the help of our unseen allies and with our tears, if need be, we can water the brave and persistent seeds of decency, justice and truth emerging through the cracks. Together we can weave a strong cloak of protection that will prevent the further unraveling of the fragile community of life. We who can still hear the wordless language of the earth and of all our kindred who dwell here, we must not turn a deaf ear.

Life on the Margins

> How beautifully leaves grow old. How full of light and
> color are their last days.
>
> John Burroughs (1837 – 1921)

The memory of our garden volunteers who have passed on is rekindled every spring as the seeds they planted bloom again, blessing us with a beautiful reminder of life's cycle of renewal.

Glen Burleson: A font of garden wisdom. The garden spirits dance among your daylilies.

Edwin Gonzales: The bees and butterflies still visit your perennial blooms.

Barbara Gravelle: You were with us from the beginning. May the Lilac breezes carry you on.

Betty McElveen: The chimes you hung in the gardens still sing in the wind.

Martha McKeon: Yours was the first eggplant grown in the gardens, a purple gem!

Vivian Grace Novia: A wise spirit. Your red flowering Cypress vine still climbs and blooms.

Roberta Perry: Your wildflowers brightened the fence line and enlivened the garden.

Peruvio: You left us tokens of appreciation with your colorfully woven *ojo de dios* to decorate our memorial wall.

Joe Wakefield: Builder of birdhouses. You were a faithful friend and inspiration, and at 95 our eldest gardener.

Hugh Williamson: The yellow rose you planted blooms yearly along the front fence.

Jacque Wuelling: You wheeled around the garden in your electric wheelchair, encouraging our progress with the accessible pathway.

From the Guestbook: Reflections on Beauty and Peace

"So much love pouring into this little space and from and between these people. A joy to witness."

"There is so much beauty here… I miss my garden at home, but this community garden gives me peace and joy. Plants connect us all."

"Such a hidden gem… Plants are the past, present and future."

"Are flowers not the stars of the earth? Thank you for sharing this with the community."

"There is nothing like the beauty of nature to bring you into the present moment. So grateful for this little haven. Be here now."

"Your garden is like a fairy dreamland. It is so peaceful here. I love it. Thank you for sharing it with this community."

"Thank you for creating such a beautiful respite. I am so happy to have discovered this magical spot and will definitely return."

"What an amazing inspiring place! Love this spot and the promise it holds."

"In a stroke of pure serendipity, we stumbled upon your community garden. It is a profound joy to feel so welcome and to join in your whimsy."

"What a beautiful urban garden! The variety of plants and the care that has gone into maintaining it is inspiring. Keep it up!"

Local Voices

"I'm a resident at the Vanderbilt for seniors—lived there for 23 years. Your garden has always been a source of inspiration… Thank you for your excellent community contribution."

"I have lived in and around Asheville my entire 40 years of life, and I am refreshed and very grateful to see people preserving such a lovely and meaningful space."

"From not so far, but so pleased to find this kind tending of green things… The trees shall clap their hands."

"The world needs more community gardens. Thank you for planting the seeds."

"Elder & Sage. Thank you for existing. I am a local who works downtown, and this magical garden is my favorite place to enjoy breakfast and coffee each morning."

Visitors from Afar

"My partner and I come to this garden every time we're in town. A lot is happening in the world, it's scary and unpredictable. But it is also beautiful. – Desiree, Ft. Bragg, NC "

"We came to Asheville on vacation and stumbled upon this beautiful garden."

"Drove in from Tampa, Florida with my mom and stumbled upon this gorgeous garden!"

"Jackpot! On a spontaneous road trip from Greenville, SC…"

"I traveled from China. Very impressed by this beautiful garden."

"I traveled from Sebring, Florida. Love to garden. I received some great ideas. Great job. Continue growing."

"Our first visit to Asheville and we discovered your charming garden. Thank you for greening our world."

"This was an unexpected find for us. Many people appreciate the dedication this must take."

"On a girls' trip from Georgia. We just saw a sign and stopped by and met the most friendly people ever!"

"I passed by and had to stop in. Chef from South Florida, recently started a community garden in my hometown."

Delia, Weston, Florida – "What a treasure you have here! We hope it endures."

Chris, West Virginia – "A teetotally original, spontaneous, and yet so well maintained."

Community and Connection

"Site of such radical care and nurturing. So important for the community and the world." – Visiting from Greeneville, Tennessee

"It is clear talking to those who volunteer here that it is a highly valued space, one that promotes togetherness and green space in an otherwise barren urban environment."

"What a beautiful little spot in Asheville city proper. We stumbled upon the greenery during an urban walking tour… Awesome to see a community come together."

"What a treasure! Exploring the area and discovered this garden full of positive energy!"

"Please don't shut down this beautiful community garden. We need more nature and light in this dark, money-driven world."

"Such a beautiful garden and even more lovely people. Thank you for this hidden, wholesome gem."

"A year into the pandemic we decided to finally get away… There is so much beauty here… I miss my garden at home, but this community garden gives me peace and joy… COVID can't take away our spirits."

"The concept of a public space made by all citizens is a way to bring nature to the mind of people."

> **The beauty of nature is often the wisest balm, for it gently relieves and releases the caged mind.**
> —John O'Donohue

Endnotes

1   Aldo Leopold, *A Sand County Almanac and Sketches Here and There* (New York: Oxford University Press, 1949), 224.

2   Phillip Gerard, "The 1980s: The City That Almost Wasn't," *Our State*. https://www.ourstate.com/the-1980s-the-city-that-almost-wasn't.

3   https://specialcollections.buncombenc.gov/2016/04/20/the-fight-to-save-11-acres-of-downtown/

4   Thomas Calder, "In Photos: Over 200 line the streets for wrap the woods pop up," *Mountain Xpress*, September 6, 2025. https://mountainx.com/news/community-news/in-photos-over-200-line-the-streets-for-wrap-the-woods-pop-up/

5   Thomas Calder, "In Photos: Over 200 line the streets for wrap the woods pop up," *Mountain Xpress*, September 6, 2025. https://mountainx.com/news/community-news/in-photos-over-200-line-the-streets-for-wrap-the-woods-pop-up/

6   Clare Hanrahan, "Tear Down That Fence," *Asheville Citizen-Times*, May 24, 2015. https://www.citizen-times.com/story/opinion/2015/05/24/tear-fence/27879581/

7   Clare Hanrahan, "Staking our Claim: Asheville Citizens Reclaim Public Commons," Asheville on the Ground, June 24, 2008. Asheville On The Ground.

8   Virginia Daffron, "This Bud's For You: Grassroots Campaign Cultivates Beauty, Community," *Mountain Xpress*, 2015.

9   Cecil Bothwell, "Cecil Bothwell: Half a park? Not enough," *Asheville Citizen-Times*, April 9, 2017.

10 Tear Down That Fence.

11 Carrie Eidson, "Think small, grow big: Urban farming, without the farm," *Mountain Xpress*, July 16, 2014.

12 Rebecca Bowe, "The MAGIC of yesteryear," *Mountain Xpress*, July 19, 2006.

13 Hannah Wittman, "Food sovereignty: An inclusive model for feeding the world and cooling the planet," *One Earth*, Volume 6, Issue 5, 2023, Pp.474-478.

14 Elizabeth Eubanks. https://www.youtube.com/watch?v=fNAIwNK-88s.

15 Madeline Hackett, "Community Garden Temporarily Uprooted in Asheville but Gardeners Continue to Plant," WYFF (Greenville, SC), April 10, 2020.

16 https://www.facebook.com/PageAveAVL

17 Mackensy Lunsford, "Elder & Sage Community Gardening Group Nurtures Life on a Gravel Lot," *Asheville Citizen-Times*, July 2, 2017.

18 Tiffany Welsh, "Asheville Edibles: A Gravel Lot in the Heart of Downtown Is Getting a Lot Greener Thanks to a Partnership Between the City of Asheville and a Local Group of Gardeners," *Food Life Mag*, August 21, 2017.

19 Deborah Holt Noel, "Boomers," NC Weekend, PBS North Carolina.

20 Brenda Hughes, *Act Two Stories, Reinventing the Second Act of Life*, "Community Gardens in the City," Wetbird Productions, 2019.

21 Helen Chickering, "From Gravel to Garden of Possibilities," Blue Ridge Public Radio, June 5, 2017.

22 David LaMotte, *You Are Changing the World*, Chalice Press, 2023, p. 105.

23 David Forbes, "Thick as Thieves," *The Asheville Blade*, June 25, 2019.

24 Yuqing Pan, "The U.S. Cities That Are Gentrifying the Fastest—You'll Never Guess No. 1," Realtor.com, January 23, 2017.

25 Brooke Randle, "Asheville's Rodent Activity Concerns Residents, Officials," *Mountain Xpress*, October 26, 2018.

26 Kelly Doty, "Bear Family strolls through North Carolina City," WLOS, October 20, 2023.

27 Allison Sherman, "Helene Heroes—Ponkho Bermejo, BeLoved Asheville," *WNC Magazine*, February, 2025.

28 David Miller, "Understanding the Link Between Tourism and Asheville growth," Frontstatement.com, September 21, 2025.

29 David LaMotte, *You Are Changing the World*, Chalice Press, 2023, p. 105.

30 Stephen Wing, "The Roots Go Down into theGround," https://www.stephenwing.com.